Pagan P[ortals]
&
Shaman Pa[thways]

...an ever-growing library of shared knowledge.

Moon Books has created two unique series where leading authors and practitioners come together to share their knowledge, passion and expertise across the complete Pagan spectrum. If you would like to contribute to either series, our proposal procedure is simple and quick, just visit our website (www.MoonBooks.net) and click on Author Inquiry to begin the process.

If you are a reader with a comment about a book or a suggestion for a title we'd love to hear from you! You can find us at facebook.com/MoonBooks or you can keep up to date with new releases etc on our dedicated Portals page at facebook.com/paganportalsandshamanpathways/

'Moon Books has achieved that rare feat of being synonymous with top-quality authorship AND being endlessly innovative and exciting.'
Kate Large, Pagan Dawn

Pagan Portals

Animal Magic, Rachel Patterson
An introduction to the world of animal magic and working with animal spirit guides

Australian Druidry, Julie Brett
Connect with the magic of the southern land, its seasons, animals, plants and spirits

Blacksmith Gods, Pete Jennings
Exploring dark folk tales and customs alongside the magic and myths of the blacksmith Gods through time and place

Brigid, Morgan Daimler
Meeting the Celtic Goddess of Poetry, Forge, and Healing Well

By Spellbook & Candle, Mélusine Draco
Why go to the bother of cursing, when a bottling or binding can be just as effective?

By Wolfsbane & Mandrake Root, Mélusine Draco
A study of poisonous plants, many of which have beneficial uses in both domestic medicine and magic

Candle Magic, Lucya Starza
Using candles in simple spells, seasonal rituals and essential craft techniques

Celtic Witchcraft, Mabh Savage
Wield winds of wyrd, dive into pools of wisdom; walk side by side with the Tuatha Dé Danann

Dancing with Nemetona, Joanna van der Hoeven
An in-depth look at a little-known Goddess who can help bring peace and sanctuary into your life

Fairy Witchcraft, Morgan Daimler
A guidebook for those seeking a path that combines modern Neopagan witchcraft with the older Celtic Fairy Faith

God-Speaking, Judith O'Grady
What can we do to save the planet? Three Rs are not enough. Reduce, reuse, recycle...and religion

Gods and Goddesses of Ireland,
Meet the Gods and Goddesses of Pagan Ireland in myth and modern practice

Grimalkyn: The Witch's Cat, Martha Gray
A mystical insight into the cat as a power animal

Hedge Riding, Harmonia Saille
The hedge is the symbolic boundary between the two worlds and this book will teach you how to cross that hedge

Hedge Witchcraft, Harmonia Saille
Learning by experiencing is about trusting your instincts and connecting with your inner spirit

Hekate, Vivienne Moss
The Goddess of Witches, Queen of Shades and Shadows, and the ever-eternal Dark Muse haunts the pages of this poetic devotional, enchanting those who love Her with the charm only this Dark Goddess can bring

Runes, Kylie Holmes
The Runes are a set of 24 symbols that are steeped in history, myths and legends. This book offers practical and accessible information for anyone to understand this ancient form of divination

Sacred Sex and Magick, Web PATH Center
Wrap up ecstasy in love to create powerful magick, spells and healing

Spirituality without Structure, Nimue Brown
The only meaningful spiritual journey is the one you consciously undertake

The Awen Alone, Joanna van der Hoeven
An introductory guide for the solitary Druid

The Cailleach, Rachel Patterson
Goddess of the ancestors, wisdom that comes with age, the weather, time, shape-shifting and winter

The Morrigan, Morgan Daimler
On shadowed wings and in raven's call, meet the ancient Irish Goddess of war, battle, prophecy, death, sovereignty, and magic

Urban Ovate, Brendan Howlin
Simple, accessible techniques to bring Druidry to the wider public

Your Faery Magic, Halo Quin
Tap into your Natural Magic and become the Fey you are

Zen Druidry, Joanna van der Hoeven
Zen teachings and Druidry combine to create a peaceful life
path that is completely dedicated to the here and now

Shaman Pathways

Aubry's Dog, Melusine Draco
A practical and essential guide to using canine magical energies

Black Horse White Horse, Mélusine Draco
Feel the power and freedom as Black Horse, White Horse
guides you down the magical path of this most noble animal

Celtic Chakras, Elen Sentier
Tread the British native shaman's path, explore the Goddess
hidden in the ancient stories; walk the Celtic chakra spiral
labyrinth

Druid Shaman, Danu Forest
A practical guide to Celtic shamanism with exercises and
techniques as well as traditional lore for exploring the Celtic
Otherworld

Elen of the Ways, Elen Sentier
British shamanism has largely been forgotten: the reindeer
Goddess of the ancient Boreal forest is shrouded in mystery...
follow her deer-trods to rediscover her old ways

Following the Deer Trods, Elen Sentier
A practical handbook for anyone wanting to begin the old
British paths. Follows on from Elen of the Ways

Trees of the Goddess, Elen Sentier
Work with the trees of the Goddess and the old ways of Britain

Way of the Faery Shaman, Flavia Kate Peters
Your practical insight into Faeries and the elements they engage
to unlock real magic that is waiting to help you

Web of Life, Yvonne Ryves
A new approach to using ancient ways in these contemporary
and often challenging times to weave your life path

What people are saying about

Pagan portals: The Dagda

Another outstanding book from the very talented Morgan Daimler. This Pagan Portal gives an introduction to the intriguing god, Dagda. Morgan has covered not just the mythology and associations but also drawn from her own experiences and reflected upon Dagda in the modern world. The book also includes some beautiful invocations and prayers.

Rachel Patterson, author of *The Cailleach, Witchcraft into the Wilds* and the Kitchen Witchcraft series

I cannot recommend this book highly enough. While short, as all Pagan Portals titles are, it presents information, both familiar and very unfamiliar, in an immensely accessible and appealing way. It is so evocative as to seemingly convey the essence of the Dagda in its pages. It is immensely well-written, which helps it achieve its goals, and makes it a joy to read in itself. It marks another triumph for Morgan Daimler.

Segomâros Widugeni, author at Nemeton Segomâros

Many Irish goddesses have become increasingly popular within modern Paganism, but sadly many of the myths and stories of their male counterparts are ignored. In her latest instalment in the Pagan Portal series Morgan Daimler has created the essential guide to the Dagda. It is the perfect balance of scholarly resources and practical advice for modern seekers

Stephanie Woodfield, author of *Celtic Lore & Spellcraft of the Dark Goddess*, and *Dark Goddess Craft*

I've held The Dagda in my affections for many years and this is the first book which clearly explains the complexity of this important Irish god. Daimler takes us on a journey through the richness of his mythology, history, his many names & titles as well as suggesting prayers and rituals which honour him. I thoroughly recommend *Pagan Portals: The Dagda* to those who are curious and to those who want to deepen their knowledge and connection to the Good God of Ireland.

Jane Brideson, artist and Blogger at The Ever-Living Ones

Pagan Portals

The Dagda

Meeting the Good God of Ireland

Pagan Portals

The Dagda

Meeting the Good God of Ireland

Morgan Daimler

Winchester, UK
Washington, USA

First published by Moon Books, 2018
Moon Books is an imprint of John Hunt Publishing Ltd., No. 3 East St., Alresford,
Hampshire SO24 9EE, UK
office1@jhpbooks.net
www.johnhuntpublishing.com
www.moon-books.net

For distributor details and how to order please visit the 'Ordering' section on our website.

Text copyright: Morgan Daimler 2017

ISBN: 978 1 78535 640 7
978 1 78535 641 4 (ebook)
Library of Congress Control Number: 2017960350

A CIP catalogue record for this book is available from the British Library.

Design: Stuart Davies

Printed and bound by CPI Group (UK) Ltd, Croydon, CR0 4YY, UK

We operate a distinctive and ethical publishing philosophy in
all areas of our business, from our global network of authors to
production and worldwide distribution.

Contents

This book is dedicated to all the people trying to preserve the old ways and mythology, who keep the stories alive by telling them and by creating new ones built on the old.
With immense thanks to the friends on social media who helped me suss out some of the ways the Dagda is showing up in modern contexts including video games.

Preface

The Irish Goddesses tend to get more attention than the Gods in modern paganism but of those Gods, the Dagda is one of the most popular. Despite this it can be very difficult to find solid resources about him and often he shows up only as a small section in books taking on the subject of the Irish or Celtic Gods more generally. *Pagan Portals: The Dagda* was written as a resource for seekers of the Dagda specifically and offers both solid academic material and practical advice on connecting with him in a format that is accessible and designed to be easy to read, although it does contain a lot of academic references to older mythology. It is meant to be a basic introduction to this deity and also a bridge for beginners to feel more comfortable as they seek to learn more about this powerful but enigmatic God before moving forward.

In writing this I have drawn on many different sources and have carefully referenced and cited all of them. My own degree is in psychology so I prefer to use the APA method of citations. This means that within the text after quotes or paraphrased material the reader will see a set of parenthesis containing the author's last name and date the source was published; this can then be cross referenced with the bibliography at the end of the book. I find this method to be a good one and I prefer it over footnotes or other methods of citation which is why it's the one I use. I have also included endnotes in some places where a point needs to be expanded on or further discussed but where it would be awkward to do that within the text itself.

While this book can and does serve as a stand-alone work, ideally, I hope that the reader will be drawn to learn more and decide to continue seeking. The Dagda is a complex deity and no single book, of any length, can entirely capture his layers and depth. To help readers use this book as a stepping stone towards further connection I have provided a list of both the references

I used in my writing and also of recommended further reading at the end of the book under the bibliography. I have tried to offer books which represent an array of options for people with different viewpoints and approaches to honouring the Dagda. I would note, however, that as far as I know at the time of writing, there is no other full-length book written exclusively on the Dagda, although I am aware of a possible anthology for him that is in the works. Most readers who are seeking to learn more about the Dagda will need to research the original myths for themselves as well as looking for what material can be found piecemeal in more modern books on Irish or Celtic paganism.

As I have said before in my previous book *Pagan Portals: The Morrigan*, I do not think that the religious framework we use to connect to the Gods matters as much as the effort to honour the old Gods itself. I think we can all do this respectfully and with an appreciation for history without the need for any particular religion. Whether we are Reconstructionists, Wiccans or Celtic pagans; all that really matter is that we are approaching our faith with sincerity and a genuine intention. To that end this book is written without any specific spiritual faith in mind, beyond polytheism, and it is up to the reader to decide how best to incorporate the material. My own personal path is rooted in witchcraft and reconstruction; that is bound to colour some of my opinions in the text, however, so the reader may want to keep that in mind.

I have been an Irish-focused pagan since 1991 and have long held a deep respect for the Dagda in my worship as a giver of abundance and wisdom. Although he is not one of the primary Gods I honour, he is an important one. For some people this book may be the first step in a lifelong journey, the first attempt to reach out to this important and complex God. For others, this book may simply provide a greater understanding of the Dagda, his history, and modern beliefs and practices associated with him. In either case I hope that the reader feels that some value is gained from the time spent with this little volume, getting to know the Dagda.

Chapter 1

Who Is the Dagda?

The Dagda said, 'The power which you boast, I will wield it all together.'
'You are the Dagdae!' everyone said; and 'Dagdae' [Good God] was on him from that time after.
(Cath Maige Tuired)

One of the most well-known Gods of the Tuatha Dé Danann is the Dagda, but he is also one of the most complex. Books on Celtic Gods or subjects relating to Celtic paganism often mention the Dagda, but only in passing, or repeating information that is based on information that is itself repeated from modern sources disconnected from the older mythology and folklore. The goal with this book is not only to provide a more in-depth introduction to the Dagda for readers but also to get back to the original source material and listen to what that material is telling us. The first place to start in understanding the Dagda then is to begin by looking at his most well-known name as well as his many other by-names and epithets and investigate what those names can tell us about him.

Name and Cognates

The Dagda can be found under many variations of the name, such as Daghdae, Dagdai, Daghdo, Daghdou, Dagdae, Dagdhua, Dagdhae, (eDIL, 2017). Usually the definitive article 'the' is added before Dagda so that we call him the Dagda instead of just Dagda. The name Dagda itself is an epithet which means 'Good God', implying a God good at all things.[1] This name is gained during the second battle of Maige Tuired when he promises to do as much as all the other Tuatha Dé Danann have said they will do in the fight (Gray, 1983). This word play recurs often in other myths as well where we see him referred to by name and then called the good or excellent God.

O hOgain suggests that the name Dagda comes from the root Dago-Dewios, a cognate with other Indo-European sky gods such as Zeus, and also connects him through this and his imagery to the Gaulish Secullos (O hOgain, 2006). The Dagda is sometimes viewed as a cognate to other Indo-European gods including the aforementioned Zeus and Secullos, as well as Thor. Secullos, Thor and the Dagda are all deities who are connected to storms, specifically lightning and thunder, fertility of crops, and using a club-like weapon. Alexei Kondratiev in his article 'Basic Celtic Deity Types' explains the connection between the Dagda and Secullos, whose name means 'Good Striker', in more depth. Both Gods have a striking implement and are also associated with a cauldron, in the case of Secullos the two being combined with the cauldron on the end of the mallet or club, making Secullos's weapon comparable to the Dagda's staff, so that both Gods wield a tool that can give life at one end or death at the other (Kondratiev, 1997).

By-Names and Epithets

His by-names and epithets can also tell us a great deal about him. These include: Dagda Mór, Eochaid Ollathair, Ruad Rofessa, Aedh Alainn, and Aodh Ruadh Ro-fessa; (Gray, 1983; O hOgain, 2006). In the Metrical Dindshenchas we also see him called Dagda Dein, Dagdai Duir, Dagda Deirg, and Dagda Donn. Each of these names has its own context and meaning which gives us a greater understanding of the Dagda himself.

Dagda Mór would mean Great Dagda, while Dagda Donn might be read as Dark Dagda or possibly as connecting the Dagda with the God Donn. It is also possible in the context it appears in that Dagda Donn was meant to be read as 'noble Dagda' since donn can have that meaning as well as several others (Martin,

2008). Eochaid Ollathair is 'Horse-lord Ample Father'; Ruad Rofessa means 'Red man of Knowledge' (specifically Druidic or Occult knowledge), and Aedh Alainn is 'Fiery Lustrous One' (O hOgain, 2006). Dagda Dein is often translated as swift Dagda although it could also be read as mighty, vehement, or strong. O hOgain posits that the descriptions of him as swift may indicate that he was believed to be a God who responded quickly to his followers, and he also relates him to the sun and solar imagery (O hOgain, 2006). Dagda Duir is usually translated as stern Dagda, although the word dúr can also mean firm or resolute. In the Metrical Dindshenchas he is also called 'Dagda duilig', or hard Dagda, and Dagda druine which many mean skilful Dagda but could also be read as solid or strong Dagda (Martin, 2008).

Ollaithar is often interpreted today to mean 'All father' because people mistakenly associate the Old Irish word oll with its English homonym all. In truth oll means great, ample, or vast with connotations of both size and fame. People inclined to look at the Dagda as a more neopagan type Father God should bear in mind the actual connotations of 'Good God' as well as the more restricted translation of Ollathair, as there is no direct evidence that he was previously seen as the literal father of the Gods, but rather as prolific. Sjeostedt makes this point in her book *Celtic Gods and Heroes*, where she says: '*This epithet* [Ollaithar] *does not mean that he is in fact the father of all the other Gods; we know from the genealogies that he is not*' (Sjoestedt, 2000, p 38). It is worth noting that while the Dagda is prolific in fathering many children he is not actually the most prolific father among the Tuatha Dé Danann, nor are his children necessarily the most important among the Gods. It is possible that this emphasis on his role as a father, and this epithet of Ollaithar, ample father, is meant to demonstrate his role as a good, stable king and provider for his people.

In fairness to the view that places the Dagda as a central father-like figure, however, O hOgain suggests that the Dagda can be connected to the 'Dis Pater' father deity that Caesar claims the Gauls believed they were descended from (O hOgain, 2006). This may be somewhat reinforced by the fact that the Dagda was called Dagda Donn in one source and if we take Donn not as an adjective but as the name of the deity Donn it could support a view of the Dagda as an ancestral figure. Donn is a God who was the first Milesian to die in Ireland and now possesses the place through which all mortal dead must pass to move on to the next life. The syncretisation of the two deities, at least, may hint at a connection between with the idea of the Dagda as an ancestral God or God of the dead, which may also be supported by his association with several burial mounds.

Beyond these the text of the Cath Maige Tuired provides a long list of names for the Dagda, after he is challenged to carry a Fomorian princess on his back and replies that he has a geis (taboo) preventing him from doing so unless she knows his full name. She asks him three times for his name and on the third request he replies: '*Fer Benn Bruach Brogaill Broumide Cerbad Caic Rolaig Builc Labair Cerrce Di Brig Oldathair Boith Athgen mBethai Brightere Tri Carboid Roth Rimaire Riog Scotbe Obthe Olaithbe*' (Gray, 1983). These many names are obscure and often not translated, however, some attempts to understand them have been made and their meanings are important in understanding more about the Dagda. Fer Benn can be read as 'horned man' or 'peaked man' with fer meaning man and benn meaning horned, peaked, pointed. It may also mean man of the mountains or man of the prongs (Williams, 2016). Bruach without a fada is a word that means a border or edge, but with a fada, brúach, means large bellied; I would suggest that the second meaning is more likely. Brogaill is uncertain but may be a compound of brog and oll, perhaps meaning a great lapful (eDIL, 2017). Broumide is also uncertain but may be a compound of bró and mide, millstone and middle; although Isolde Carmody suggests it means 'farter' (Carmody, 2012). Cerbaid is a verbal noun that means to hack or cut off. Caic is a form of cacc, excrement. Rolaig is a form of leach, warrior, with ro added as an intensifier. Buile may be a form of baile, madness, or buille stroke or chime; buile may also be a form of builce meaning stomach. If the two are read together as Rolaig Buile they may perhaps be interpreted as 'great warrior of the belly' (Williams, 2016). Labair relates to being loud, noisy, boastful (Martin, 2008). Cerrce is uncertain but may possibly mean 'striker' and connect the Dagda back to other hammer wielding Gods (Martin, 2008). Di bríg is a phrase possibly meaning 'greatly worthy'; Martin asserts that it means 'God of power'. Oldathair – a form of ollathair, great or ample father. Boith is a form of baeth meaning both silly, foolish, reckless as well as wanton or sexual open. Athgen mBethai may mean 'regeneration of the world'; although this is not agreed on by all sources it is supported by the Dagda's wider mythic actions (Martin, 2008). Brightere may be a compound of bríg, valuable/powerful, and tír, territory or land. Tri Carboid Roth is uncertain but may mean three chariot wheels. Rimaire is also uncertain but could mean either 'retelling' or 'bad weather' if it is related to the word rím (eDIL, 2017). Ríog is a form of the word for king. Scotbe may relate to judgement. Isolde Carmody suggests that these three should be read together to give us 'enumerating a king's speech' or less literally enumerating judgements (Carmody, 2012). Obthe Olaithbe could mean 'refusal of the great ebb' (Carmody, 2012).

Beyond this we are also told in the Dúil Dromma Cetta that another name for the Dagda is Cera. The word is of uncertain meaning but possibly relates to the word 'cir' meaning jet (eDIL, 2017). This is the only reference I know of for this name of the Dagda, but it is something to consider. A few other miscellaneous names that appear only once in a single source are Áed Abaid, Dagan, and Cratan Cain (Gray, 1983). Áed Abaid may mean 'Fiery Very-yellow one'; Dagan is the name of a Semetic God, however, I would note that in that text it immediately states 'that is the Dagda' so it is possible that this could represent an earlier scribal error or misspelling of Dagda rather than an intentional reference to another foreign deity; Cratan is uncertain and Cain may mean fair or beautiful (eDIL, 2017).

Ultimately, the names of the Dagda show us a deeply powerful being, one who has connections to fire and earth, who is immensely large and vastly knowledgeable especially about occult matters. He is noble and kingly but also earthy in the most literal ways. He is a warrior but also a father figure who amply provides for those who look to him. His names repeatedly connect him to the imagery of fire and of wisdom but also in the crudest terms to the earth and soil and even to bodily functions. In many ways then he is a study in opposites, a deity who encompasses antithetical forces and powers.

Physical Description

Another way that we can begin to get to know the Dagda is by looking at what information we have regarding his appearance. This is not as easy as it may first appear, however, because Irish mythology often lacks the detailed physical descriptions we find elsewhere. It is not uncommon for even well-known popular deities to have few stories that include physical descriptions and when we do find these, as often as not, they focus more on what the being is wearing or is equipped with than what they themselves look like. When it comes to the Dagda our best most detailed description of him comes from one particular story where he has been sent to spy on an enemy army and it is likely that his appearance in this case is not actually his normal one, but rather was something of a disguise meant to help him pass into the enemy camp more easily. I would encourage people to keep this in mind, despite the fact that this description has become the most popular and widespread view of the Dagda out there.

The Dagda is generally described as a large man, sometimes

comically so, with a tremendous appetite and immense capacity. It was said, based on a single incident, that to make his porridge he needed 80 gallons of milk as well as several whole sheep, pigs, and goats, and that he ate this meal with a ladle large enough to hold two people lying down (Ellis, 1987). Some modern sources describe him as red-haired, possibly relating to the name Ruad Rofessa; he is most often described and shown in modern imagery with red hair. He is considered to be generous, wise, and bigger-than-life in his appetites which may be reflected in how people visualize him (O hOgain, 2006). He is often described as immensely strong and able to complete great feats such building a fort single-handedly or clearing 12 plains in a single night. Cross and Slover describe him as '*a large eyed, large thighed, noble-great, immensely tall man*' and say that he had '*a splendid garment about him*' (Cross & Slover, 1936). Martin further clarifies that he is described as slinnénach, meaning to have great shoulders (Martin, 2008). The Metrical Dindshenchas at one point say that his face is '*broader than half a plain*' (Gwynn, 1924). These physical views of him contribute to a picture of a deity that is physically large – gigantic even – wide, muscular, and usually with a generous belly.

He is usually described wearing a tunic of some sort and sometimes a cloak. In several sources his clothing is said to be grey or dun coloured (Martin, 2008). In the Cath Maige Tuired, which is the only detailed existing description of the Dagda, he is described this way: '*Unseemly was his apparel. A cape to the hollow of his two elbows. A dun tunic around him, as far as the swelling of his rump. It is, moreover, long-breasted, with a hole in the peak. Two shoes on him of horse-hide, with the hair outside*' (Stokes, 1891). Stokes' translation is the most widely read because it is in the public domain now and free online and so this is often the visual concept of the Dagda that has been passed on within paganism. But because of the time period he was writing in, he intentionally excluded some material that he found 'obscene'[2] and for that reason I would like to also add details here from another translation by Elizabeth Gray. In that version we see the same general clothing, however, we are also told that the Dagda's penis is exposed, hanging down below the hem of his tunic, just as his buttocks are exposed in the back. This was not an uncommon style of dress for the lowest classes of that time period, although scholars debate whether the description is meant to mock the Dagda in the text or to emphasize his earthiness and connection to the common man (Williams, 2016).

The picture painted, when put together, is of a large, red-haired man dressed in the fashion of an Iron Age peasant in grey or tan colours, carrying a staff, often called club.[3] I might suggest that this typical image of the Dagda, clad in a short tunic that exposes his lower half, while entirely typical of Irish styles of dress at the time for the lower classes and worth considering, is also only one possible view of him. We know that he was also a king and a warrior and while we have no explicit descriptions of him in these roles we have enough general depictions of people from that period to know what he would have looked like, and it is unlikely that he would have ruled dressed as a common labourer or fought in battle dressed as a fort-builder.

The Dagda's Relationships with Others

The Dagda is a complex deity and his relationship to other deities is also complex throughout mythology. He was the father of a variety of children, many of them also well-known deities in their own right. He was also associated with two Tuatha Dé Danann women, one as his wife and one as a lover, as well as one Fomorian woman. He had at least five brothers, several of whom are popular deities. However, like most things in Irish mythology this information is not entirely set in stone but instead we can find different versions and variations in different texts. While it's important to understand the way that the Dagda is related to various other deities it should also be kept in mind that some of this information is fluid and open to interpretation.

In most sources the Dagda is said to be the son of Elada, sometimes spelled Elatha.[4] Keating says that his mother was Ethliu, although Gray suggests that this may be an error, confusing his father's name Elatha for a feminine name (Gray, 1983). In the Lebor Gabala Erenn his brothers are said to be Ogma, Bres, Alloth, and Delbeath (MacAlister, 1941). I need to note, though, that this Bres, Bres son of Elada, does not appear to be Eochaid Bres son of Elatha the Fomorian, and this Delbeath is one of several people bearing that name, including his own grandfather, and should not be confused with any of the others. The Dagda is also sometimes said to be the brother of Nuada, although other genealogies list Nuada's father as Echtach (O hOgain, 2006). In the Cath Maige Tuired particularly, we often see the Dagda acting with Nuada, Ogma, Goibhniu, and Dian Cecht. Although not related by blood they are a main grouping of deities who appear in various combinations, and if we include Lugh, Dian Cecht's grandson, into the group we would have the six gods of the Tuatha Dé Danann who appear most often in stories and in conjunction with each other.

His children vary by source but generally his sons are said to be Aengus mac ind Óg (Aengus the young son), Cearmait Milbel (Cermait Sweet-mouth), Aodh Caem (Aedh the Fair), Conan, Midir, Bodhbh Dearg (Red Bodb), and his daughters are Adair, Ainge, and Brighid; in one later example, Dian Cecht is also said to be his son (O hOgain, 2006; Gray, 1983). Although he is better known now as a Fairy King, Finnbheara was originally one of the Tuatha Dé Danann, he is mentioned as such in the Agallamh na Seanoach, and is also said to be the youngest son of the Dagda in the Altram Tige Dá Medar. His mother, like so many of the Dagda's children's mothers, is not specified.

The trio of Aengus (alternately spelled Oengus), Aedh, and Cermait are often mentioned together in mythology. In the Lebor Gabala Erenn they are referred to as *the three sons of the Dagda* and in the Metrical Dindshanchas its said *'The hero Eochaid's [the Dagda's] three sons, who knew no hour of jealousy, were Oengus, and Aed and Cermat of the battle squadrons'*. This may indicate that this grouping had some particular importance at some point. It also reflects a pattern we occasionally see elsewhere in Irish mythology of three siblings grouped together when they are either significant or share a common power; we see this with the children of Dian Cecht, the sons of Tuireann, the three Brighids, and both groupings of the three daughters of Ernmas: Eriu, Banba, and Fotla as well as Badb, Macha, and the Morrigan.

His sons often die after trying to obtain a woman who is not available; for example, both Cermait and Aedh are killed by jealous husbands after having affairs with married women. Conan is killed in combat after asking for the maiden Celg's hand in marriage and being refused because her father had been told he would die should his daughter ever wed (Gwynn, 1924). Midir marries his second wife Etain and then loses her to the jealousy of his first wife; Etain is transformed to a fly and worm and puddle and eventually reborn as a human woman who Midir must win away from her new mortal husband. Only Aengus successfully marries the literal woman of his dreams Caer Iobharmheith and lives, as far as we know, happily with her, but even that is not easily achieved. Finnbheara is also known in folklore for his fondness of women, married or not, even though he himself was said to have a peerlessly beautiful wife named Una. This may connect the Dagda to the concept of passion or of sexual envy, and we should note that he himself fathered Aengus on another man's wife.

His most well-known daughter is certainly the Goddess Brighid. She is called the Dagda's daughter in many sources including the Lebor Gabala Erenn and the Cath Maige Tuired. Cormac's Glossary tells us that he actually has three daughters all named Brighid, one who is a healer, one a poet, and one a blacksmith. Much like his sons can be said to reflect different aspects of the Dagda's nature, we can see the same thing with Brighid who has connections to fire, warriors, justice, sovereignty, poetry, and wisdom.

Although he has a large number of children, only Aengus's mother is certain; generally while his children are named, their mother or mothers are not mentioned. He is married to the Morrigan, but was also the lover of Bóinne, despite the fact she was married to someone else. The story of his affair with Bóinne is one of his more famous tales, coming to us from the Metrical Dindshenchas but also appearing in many retellings and modern folklore. In the story he takes Bóinne, who is the wife of either Elcmar or Nechtan,[5] as his lover. In the Cath Maige Tuired he also has a sexual encounter with a Fomorian princess, the unnamed daughter of Indech, and the text tells us that she became his 'bancharoid' likely a version of the Old Irish word for concubine (carebhen) although Gray chooses to translate this as 'mistress'.

His relationship to the Morrigan is complex and deserves a bit more discussion. There is some debate particularly in modern paganism about whether or not the Dagda and the Morrigan are actually married. The bulk of evidence in mythology favours this interpretation. In the Metrical Dindshenchas, poem 49 Odras, says:

[then] the wife of the Dagda came,
a phantom the shape-shifting Goddess.
... the mighty Mórrígan,
whose ease was a host of troops.

In the story of the *Cath Maige Tuired* we see a tale related where the Dagda and Morrigan meet just before Samhain, before the battle takes place, and after the two have sex; the place they lay together is called 'The Bed of the Married Couple'. We are also told in the poem for the Brug na Boinde I:

14

Here slept a married pair
After the battle of Maige Tuired yonder
The great woman, the Dagda Donn
Not obscure is there dwelling there.

The Morrigan is not explicitly named in the second poem, but rather we are told 'in ben mór', the great woman, and it seems to be placing the famous meeting of the Morrigan and Dagda after the battle of Maige Tuired rather than before. But the second version of this poem mentions the Paps of the Morrigan, which can be seen from Sid in Broga and refers to it as 'the paps of the King's Queen' while discussing the Bed of the Dagda and also the place where his son Cermait is born. It seems clear looking at all of this evidence together that in the older view, the Morrigan and Dagda were understood as a married couple.

Each of the Kings of the Tuatha Dé Danann were married to sovereignty goddesses, if we agree with the supposition that Nuada was in fact married to Macha,[6] and it is worth considering the importance of the Dagda, in particular, being married to the Morrigan. The two are a powerful contrast and as such are an equally powerful team. The Dagda is a god of abundance, right rulership, wisdom, and magical power; the Morrigan is a goddess of battle, death, prophecy, and incitement. He is a champion and fierce warrior – she is a bringer of battle and giver of victory. He is a poet and harpist – she is a speaker of prophecy and satire. He is a king and excels even among the other Gods – she is the Great Queen and her name became a title that other goddesses would bear as well. From a more humorous point of view, he possesses a cow whose cry steals other cows away, and she is fond of stealing cows as a hobby.

Looking at the different names of the Dagda has shown us a lot about him – he is the Good God of all skills but also the Red-one of Great Knowledge and the Horseman Ample Father. He is swift, strong, and stern as well as noble. The list of his names from the *Cath Maige Tuired* shows us that he is connected to earth and earthly functions, but we see through his names that he is also associated with fire and through his stories we see his connection to the fire of physical passion. Looking at his relationships to other deities, especially his family has also shown us a great deal about the Dagda and we see many of his own characteristics reflected in his children.

Endnotes

1. English speakers should be careful not to assume that the title of 'good god' has any moral implications. Good in this case isn't meant to imply a sense of good or evil, but rather good in the sense of positive, noble, excellent; dag in Old Irish can also be an intensive meaning something roughly like 'very' in English. Dag Dia, then, 'Noble God' or 'Excellent God', hence why he is given this name after proclaiming that he can wield all the same skills as the others.

2. Stokes acknowledges these exclusions in his own notes on the text. For example, in the scene that is quoted here describing the Dagda footnote 8 states in part: '*Here is omitted an account of the meeting of the Dagdae and the daughter of Indech under difficulties caused by the distention of the Dagdae's stomach. Much of it is obscure to me, and much of the rest is too indecent to be published in this Revue*' (Stokes, 1891). The material that he found indecent includes descriptions of genitals, excrement, and sex.

3. The Dagda's staff will be discussed in greater depth later.

4. Old Irish has an irregular orthography which means that spelling is not standardized and often fluid. This is partially why we see such a wide variety of spellings for the Dagda's name and it can cause confusion when trying to sort out genealogy because sometimes it is difficult to be certain if a variation is a simple spelling change or meant to be a different name entirely. In this case the Dagda's father is

Elada, which may be spelled several ways. However, there is some uncertainty as to whether this Elada, son of Delbeath, is the same or different from the Fomorian Elada who is the father of Bres by Eriu. This confusion is not helped by the fact that there appear to be two distinct characters named Bres who are both sons of beings named Elada but who have different roles in mythology.

5. It has been suggested by some scholars that Elcmar, Nechtan and Nuada are all names for the same Deity. We see Nuada with the epithet 'Necht' and we see both Elcmar and Nechtan associated with the Brug na Boinde. Both Elcmar and Nechtan are said to have connections to the river Boyne and its ultimate source, the well of Segais.

6. Several scholars have suggested that Nuada and Macha were a married couple although the evidence supporting this idea is not straightforward. As sometimes happens, what began as academic theory has entered into some corners of modern paganism, and even lighter academia, as assumed fact, however, nowhere in mythology is this explicitly stated as we see in the above evidence for the Dagda and the Morrigan. I happen to agree with the idea myself and discuss it in my previous book *Pagan Portals: The Morrigan*.

Chapter 2

The Dagda in Mythology

The Tuatha De asked who should lead them on that day. 'I will,' said the Dagda, 'for in me you have an excellent god;' and, thereupon, he went forth with his sons and brothers.
(Fraser, Cét-Cath Maige Tuired)

The Dagda is a popular deity who appears in many different myths and older sources. It is important to look at these stories and myths and to understand the Dagda's different appearances, but we must also understand that the myths can be contradictory and we may see actions ascribed to one character in one story but to another character in a different story; in the same way the genealogies of the deities are often contradictory. When we are looking at the myths we shouldn't view them as written in stone, so to speak, but rather as stories that have been preserved and which may have variations and alternate versions to be found elsewhere. Nonetheless, to understand the Dagda we need to understand how he has been preserved in mythology over the centuries.

What follows is a selection of the main and more important stories in which the Dagda has a particularly highlighted role. These are not complete retellings of the myths nor are they meant to be full versions of the stories; rather they are highlights focusing on the Dagda's activities. Consider these the Cliff Notes version of the Irish myths centred on the Dagda, but I highly encourage everyone who is interested in these to read the original myths themselves.

Lebor Gabala Erenn

The Lebor Gabala Erenn (LGE) or Book of the Takings of Ireland, is a multi-volume set of stories about the various peoples who settled Ireland. We see the Tuatha Dé Danann appearing in volume 4 where we are given information about who the different Gods are and how they are connected to each other as well as some of their exploits. The LGE does not read like a traditional story or myth in the way that others do but in many places is more like a list of facts or information. This can make it a more difficult source to work with, particularly because it contains information that is contradictory, even, from one section to another; however it does have a lot of valuable material in it which is worth considering.

In the Lebor Gabala Erenn we learn that the Dagda possesses one of the four treasures of the Tuatha Dé Danann, a cauldron from which no one goes away unsatisfied. The LGE goes on to tell us of how the Tuatha Dé Danann arrived in Ireland and fought against the Fir Bolg, and then how they rebelled against their king, Bres, and fought against him as well as his paternal kin the Fomorians. We are given a list of the kings of the Tuatha De Danann which includes the Dagda: *'Eochu Ollathair, that is the great Dagda, son of Elada, eighty years in the kingship of Ireland. Over him did the men of Ireland make the mound of the Brug, and (over) his three sons, Oengus, Aed, and Cermad Coem'* (MacAlister, 1941). We are also told that the Dagda died after his 80 years as a king from a wound that he was dealt 120 years earlier during the Battle of Maige Tuired. This is almost certainly a later attempt by non-pagans to reconcile two stories, one of which said the Dagda was mortally wounded or killed at Maige Tuired, the other which said he was king for 80 years after Lugh's 40 years as king. According to this story in the LGE, the Dagda finally died at the Brug na Boind of a javelin wound inflicted by a Fomorian woman named Cetlenn all those years previously.

The Cét-Chath Maige Turied

The Cét-Chath Maige Tuired, or First Battle of the Plain of Pillars, is the story of how the Tuatha De Danann first came to Ireland and took the territory from the Fir Bolg. When the Tuatha De Danann initially appear in the story, the Dagda is the first to be mentioned by name: *'They had a god of wizardry of their own, Eochaid Ollathir, called the Great Dagda, for he was an excellent god'* (Fraser, 1916).

The Tuatha De Danann arrive in Ireland, landing in Connacht and burning their ships before proceeding inland. They encounter the Fir Bolg and each group sends out one man to parley so that the two sides get the measure of each other. The Tuatha De Danann say that they do not want a fight but rather prefer to divide the land equally between the two groups, but the Fir Bolg reject this idea and choose war. The Fir Bolg send an envoy to the Tuatha De Danann to discuss how the war is to be fought and the Dagda is included with the high king, Nuada, and Bres in the group who makes the Decision to fight equally matched battles each day.

The battles begin on Midsummer and the Dagda is the first to engage in the fighting, as the text tells us: *'The Dagda began the attack on the enemy by cutting his way through them to the west …'* (Fraser, 1916). That first day the Fir Bolg are victorious and drive the Tuatha Dé Danann back to their own camp. The second day of battle is a draw, with the Tuatha Dé Danann driving the Fir Bolg back but suffering great losses in the process. On the third day when the Tuatha Dé Danann need to choose who will lead them in battle the Dagda volunteers: *'"I will," said the Dagda, "for in me you have an excellent god"'* (Fraser, 1916). Here we see a common play on words with the Dagda because his name can be read as 'good God' or 'excellent God'. In this battle the Dagda kills the Fir Bolg hero Cirb. For the second day in a row the two groups end in a draw. The fourth day sees a great battle in which many warriors fall and where Nuada loses his shield arm to the Fir Bolg champion Sreng; when that happens, it is the Dagda along with the warrior Aengaba who comes to his defence. The

Dagda stands over the fallen king and drives off the Fir Bolg, saving his life. After this the Dagda's brother Bres (not the same Bres who would later be king of the Tuatha Dé Danann) is killed and the Dagda and his remaining brothers fight to avenge him. The Dagda recounts all of the events of the battle up to that point to Nuada.

The Fir Bolg king and his son are killed and finally the last one left fighting against the Tuatha Dé Danann is the champion Sreng who had struck of Nuada's arm. He returns to fight against Nuada again, challenging him to single combat, but refuses to tie one of his arms to allow a fair fight. Because of this, and not wanting to lose their king, the Tuatha Dé Danann offers the Fir Bolg the province of Connacht and the two groups make peace.

The Cath Maige Tuired

The Cath Maige Tuired, or Battle of the Plain of Pillars, is the story of the Tuatha Dé Danann overthrowing their king Bres and fighting against Bres's paternal relatives, the Fomorians. It's one of the more important stories in the Mythological Cycle and the Dagda appears throughout in different ways. It is also one of the most comprehensive myths we have and quite a lot occurs throughout the story. It is worth reading the myth in full at some point, and I encourage readers to do so if possible.

Initially we see the Dagda in a difficult position. Bres, who is the son of a Tuatha Dé Danann mother and Fomorian father has been named king after Nuada was maimed in battle, but is proving to be a poor king. He is taxing the Tuatha Dé Danann, is inhospitable, and is forcing the champions of the Tuatha Dé into menial labour. To this end he has the Dagda build a fort for him, and each night the Dagda's food is taken from him by Cridenbel a blind satirist. In this state of distress, Aengus comes to his father and suggests a plan to be free of the satirist, whereby he gives the Dagda three pieces of gold to put in his food. Since the satirist asks each night to be given the three best portions of the

Dagda's meal he will be given the bits with the gold in them, which will kill him. The Dagda would then be accused of the murder but Aengus says that if he contests the king's judgement and explains that he did not poison the satirist with an herb but gave him what he asked for – the best of his portion of food which happened that day to have gold pieces in it – the king will have to find him innocent. This comes to pass and when it is shown that the gold is in Cridenbel's stomach, the Dagda is found innocent.

Next, Aengus again goes to his father and tells him that when his work building the fort is finished he should ask for one specific cow as his reward. Bres mocks this choice, but there is wisdom and trickery in it as this cow is one who all the other cattle of Ireland will follow.

A rebellion is eventually fomented because of Bres's bad kingship and inhospitality, encouraged by the healing of Nuada's arm. When Bres is asked to step down as king he responds by asking for time, and goes to his father's people to raise an army to fight for his throne. In turn, the Tuatha Dé Danann gather to discuss their own battle plans. During this meeting Nuada asks each what they can contribute to the fight, and three specific groups respond: the sorcerer, the cupbearers, and the Druids. After all have pledged their powers to fight against Bres and the Fomorians, the Dagda utters the famous line that he himself will wield all the powers that the others have promised, to which they proclaim him the 'dag dia' or good/excellent God, and the text says that this is how he earned the name Dagda.

The group separates, agreeing to meet again in a certain number of years, and goes to prepare. The Dagda, Lugh and Ogma go to the three Gods of Danu[1] who help outfit Lugh for the battle.

We are then told that the Dagda has a house in the north. The Dagda goes to meet the Morrigan at a pre-arranged time and place, near the river Unshin around Samhain;[2] on the particular occasion of the meeting that year, this occurs near the time of the battle. He finds her straddling the river with her hair unbound washing her genitals, and the text tells us that the two talk and then unite. Afterwards she gives him advice about the battle to come and promises that she herself will go and use magic against the Fomorian king, Indech, bringing two handfuls of blood to show the army of the Tuatha De Danann.

Next, we see Lugh, who has been given charge of the Gods by Nuada, sending the Dagda out to spy among the Fomorians. The Dagda goes to the Fomorian camp under a truce and they mock his reputation for having a huge appetite by digging a great pit and filling it with porridge for him to eat. He was told that they would kill him if he failed to eat the entire amount, because they would see it as an insult to their hospitality, and so he took his great spoon which could fit a man and woman lying down together in it and ate everything before him. He cleaned the entire trench down to the gravel at the bottom, and his stomach then was as huge as a cauldron; the Fomorians laughed at his appearance.

He went away from the enemy camp and after a short time came upon a Fomorian Princess[4] who demanded he carry her on his back. The two physically fought and went back and forth verbally sparring until the girl persuaded the Dagda to tell her both his full name[3] and also to relieve himself, clearing his bowels after his copious meal. He carries her on his back and the two become lovers, after which the Fomorian tries to keep the Dagda from going to the battle. She promises to be a stone in every ford, barring his way; he replies that every stone will bear the mark of his foot. She promises to be *'a giant oak in every ford and every pass'* that he will cross; he replies that every oak will bear the mark of his axe from that time on (Gray, 1983). At this the woman reverses her promises and instead tells him to let the Fomorians come into the land and says she will work magic against them saying *'she would sing spells against them, and she would practice the Deadly art of the wand against them – and she alone would take on a ninth part of the host'* (Gray, 1983).

Now we see Lugh asking the Tuatha De Danann, as Nuada had previously, what they will bring to the battle and there follows a long list of responses from different beings. Again the Dagda is the last to answer, this time giving a more precise response, saying: *'I will fight for the men of Ireland with mutual smiting and Destruction and wizardy. Their bones under my club will soon be as many hailstones under the feet of herds of horses, where the double enemy meets on the battlefield of Mag Tuired'* (Gray, 1983).

The battle was joined and after hard fighting, the Tuatha Dé Danann eventually prevailed and defeated the Fomorians. We see the Dagda appearing again after the fighting is over when we are told that his harpistr and harp have been stolen by the retreating Fomorians. Lugh, Ogma and the Dagda follow in order to recover them. They reach a banqueting hall where Bres, his father, and the other Fomorians have gone and the Dagda summons his harp to him by calling out:

Come Duar Dá Bláo,
Come Cóir Cetharchair,
Come summer, come winter,
Mouth of harps and bags an pipes! (Gray, 1983)

The harp flew from its place hung on a wall, killing nine people, and returned to the Dagda who then played the three famous strains of music on it, ending with sleep music. Having put everyone in the hall to sleep, the Tuatha Dé Danann all escape. The Dagda also brings away all the cows that the Fomorians had previously taken as part of their taxing of the Tuatha Dé Danann, by using the heifer that Bres had given him in payment for his work. When this one cow called her calf, all the cows in Ireland followed her.

The Four Jewels of the Tuatha De Danann

The Four Jewels of the Tuatha De Danann is both prose and poetry; it discusses the four treasures of the Tuatha Dé Danann in more detail, including more about where the treasures came from and the four druids who taught the Gods magic. We are told again that the Dagda possesses the great cauldron and that no one went away from it 'displeased', here it is called the champion's cauldron. We are told that:

Out of Murias, a vast, great treasure, [was brought]
The Cauldron of the Dagda of heroic deeds. (Daimler, 2015)

Every time the Dagda's cauldron is mentioned it is always emphasized that it feeds all who come to it, an interesting treasure for a deity who himself is associated with hospitality and abundance. Two of the other treasures also belong to members of the Tuatha Dé Danann who are kings over the gods at different points: Nuada, who possesses the sword from which none escape once it's drawn, and Lugh who has the spear of victory, against which none can sustain battle. The fourth treasure belongs to no individual but rather to Ireland herself and that is the Lia Fal, the stone of Ireland, which cries out under the rightful king. It is certainly worth contemplating that the two other kings of the Gods who possess treasures own martial items, that one way or another ensure victory in battle; but the Dagda owns an item that does no harm to anyone but rather provides for all who are in need.

The Taking of the Sidhe

This is a crucial story but it is also one for which we have two main versions; in one version it is the Dagda that is the main actor while in the other it is Manannán mac Lir. Here, of course, we will be looking at the version which focuses on the Dagda, however, I wanted to point out that the other versions exist as well.

In the story of the Taking of the Sidhe, called De Gabail in t-Side in Irish, the Tuatha Dé Danann have just been defeated by the Milesians. Although they have lost the fight, the Gods still have power and this is demonstrated by the failure of the Milesians' cows to give milk or crops to flourish. In response they go to the Dagda and seek, as the text says, to have his friendship. An agreement is reached through the Dagda whereby the humans will give a portion of their crops and milk to the Gods and the Gods will ensure that the crops and milk – the 'ith and blicht' – are abundant.

Instead of fleeing from Ireland entirely, the Gods choose to go into the sidhe, or fairy mounds. The Dagda divides up the available sidhe among the gods, assigning each one a home (or several) throughout the island. When all of the places have been portioned out, his son Aengus comes to him and says that he alone wasn't given a new home. The Dagda replies that there are none left to be given so his son asks if he might stay in Brug na Boind for a day and a night. The Dagda agrees and goes off leaving Aengus to enjoy the hospitality of the Brug. When he returns the next day, however, and asks the return of his home Aengus refuses saying that he was given the place for a day and a night and that all of a person's life is spent in a day and a night, so, the Brug na Boind is his. Because of this verbal trickery he wins the place for his own home.

In alternate versions the Brug belongs to his mother's husband Elcmar (or Nechtan) and it is the Dagda who advises Aengus on how to trick the rightful owner out of possession of it so that he may have it.

The Wooing of Etain

An alternate version in places to the above myth, the beginning of the story of Etain describes how Aengus is conceived. In this version of the story the Dagda is king and desires Bóinne, the wife of Elcmar. She returns his feelings but won't act on them because of her husband. To engage in this affair the Dagda sends Elcmar off on an errand, but Elcmar promises to return with the day. So the Dagda uses his skill and magic to cause nine months to pass in the space of that single day, and ensures that Elcmar feels neither hunger nor thirst. While he is gone the Dagda and Bóinne have sex and a child is conceived who is then gestated and born on the same day while time is suspended, so that when Elcmar returns, he finds nothing amiss. This child is named Aengus mac Óg, or Aengus the young son. The Dagda gives the baby to Midir to be raised.

Eventually Aengus asks who his parents are and that Midir bring him to meet his father. This is done and Aengus asks that he be given land, but the Dagda explains that the place he wants to give him is already occupied – the Brug na Boind which is owned by Elcmar. He then explains how Aengus can obtain the place through trickery by going to Elcmar on Samhain, a day of peace, and threatening him with a sword unless he relinquishes the Brug. The Dagda explains that Aengus should ask for a day and night as ruler of the place and then refuse to leave as all time passes in a day and a night, which Aengus does. The matter is then brought before the king which is of course the Dagda himself who rules in Aengus's favour but gives Elcmar a new home in exchange for his old one.

Later in the story we see the Dagda appearing again when Aengus goes to him for help in acquiring the maiden Etain as a wife for Midir. Etain's father, Ailill, has said he will only agree to the marriage if certain conditions are met, including that 12 plains be cleared and then that 12 rivers be created to clear out bogs and swamps and marshland. In both cases the Dagda accomplishes the tasks in a single night, creating the 12 plains and then the 12 rivers so that Aengus can bring back the maiden to Midir.

How the Dagda Got his Staff

This story begins with the Death of the Dagda's son, Cermait, who had been caught by Lugh having an affair with the other god's wife. Lugh killed Cermait in retaliation and in his grief the Dagda preserved his son's body with frankincense, myrrh, and various unnamed herbs and began wandering the earth seeking a way to revivify him. Eventually in his travels he met three brothers who each bore a treasure: a staff that could heal at one end and kill at the other, a shirt that would grant the wearer perfect health, and a cloak that allows the wearer to choose any appearance. The three brothers were disagreeing about how to divide these treasures, which they had inherited from their father, among themselves and the Dagda asked to hold the staff. As soon as he had it he struck the three brothers with the deadly end and his son with the life-giving end, but after Cermait was revived he questioned the honour of this action. So, the Dagda healed the three brothers who then complained about being slain in that manner. The Dagda convinced them to give him the loan of the staff, offering them the sun, moon, sea and land as sureties and then advised them on how to divide the remaining two treasures among themselves.

Oengus's Dream

The Aislinge Oenguso, Aengus's Dream, is a story that primarily tells the tale of the god Aengus, his love of a woman he meets in his dreams, and his ensuing quest to find her in the waking world. Although the story is mainly Aengus's the Dagda does play a role in it and it is worth looking at a summary of his actions.

The tale starts with Aengus being visited by a mysterious woman at night who vanishes in the morning. This continues over the course of one year and he falls into a love-sickness, so help is asked of the druid Fíngen. When that isn't successful they go next to Aengus's mother Bóinne, and she also tries to help him without success. Fíngen than suggests that they go to the Dagda; the Dagda asks what help he can be if Bóinne has failed as he proclaims her knowledge equal to his own. Fíngen says that the Dagda is king of all the sidhe of Ireland and that he can send someone to Bodb[5] who it was thought might have a solution. The Dagda agrees to do this and in turn Bodb agrees to help. After a year he sends word for the Dagda and Aengus to come to him at Sidhe al Femen to identify the girl he thinks he has found. He warns Aengus, though, that even if he does recognise the young woman, Bodb has no power to make a match between them.

It turns out that the woman is named Caer and she is the daughter of Ethail a king of the sidhe in Connacht and someone who the Dagda has no power over. Bodb suggests that the Dagda go to Connacht and speak to Ailill and Medb[6] and seek their help in the matter which the Dagda then does. Ailill and Medb initially say that they cannot help but the Dagda suggests sending a message to Ethail; the king of the Connacht sidhe refuses to talk. In responses Ailill and Medb attack his sidhe and carry him off as a captive. This accomplishes nothing, though, as Ethail tells them that he has no power over his daughter. He admits that she spends one year in human form and the next in the shape of a swan and that she changed from one to the other at a certain lake at Samhain each year.

The Dagda then made peace with Ethail and eventually there was even friendship between the Dagda, Ethail and Ailill, despite what had happened. The Dagda went back to Aengus and related what he had learned, advising him to go to the lake on that Samhain and wait there for Caer.

Aengus follows this advice and joins Caer as a swan, the two flying to the Brug na Boind together the next day.

Coir Anmann

The Coir Anmann, or 'Fitness of Names', is a text that lists a variety of different mythic characters along with a few lines describing them. Although each entry is short, it's worth noting this source because it is useful in telling us new information about deities or expanding on what we may already know. The entry on the Dagda is short enough that I can include it here along with a translation:

150 Dagda .i. dagh de .i. día soinemhail ag na geintíbh é, ar do adhradháis Tuatha De Danann dó, ar bá día talmhan dóibh é ar mhét a chumachta.

151 Eochaid Ollathair .i. uilliu é inna a athair. N[ó] ollathair .i. athair oll do Thuathaibh De Danann é.

152 Ruadh Rofesa .i. is aigi robhoí óighi ind fessa g[e]inntlidhe, & is aigi bádar na tréidhe ildealbhaidhe.

(Stokes & Windisch, 1897)

150 Dagda that is a good god that is an excellent god he was of the pagans; because the Tuatha Dé Danann adored/worshiped him, because he was a god of the world to them, because of the greatness of his power.

151 Eochaid Ollathair that is greater he than his father. Or ollathair that is ample father for the Tuatha Dé Danann.

152 Ruadh Rofesa that is it was he who had the wholeness of heathen knowledge, and it is he who had the multi-formed accomplishments.

(Trans. Daimler, 2017)

Stokes offers a slightly different translation from my own (above) giving '.i. dagh de' as 'that is "fire of God"', which, although it inserts an oddly Christian connotation to the Dagda's name, does reinforce a connection between himself and fire.

Metrical Dindshenchas

The Dagda appears or is mentioned in several of the Dindshenchas, stories about the naming of places. I cannot mention all of them here or include them all, however, I do want to include at least one which is particularly significant in the Dagda's mythology. This is the Dindshenchas of Mag Muirthemne:

> *Mag Muirthemne, whence the name? Not hard to say. The sea covered it thirty years after the Flood, and hence it is called Muirthemne, that is, 'darkness of the sea', or 'it is under the sea's roof'. Or there was a magic sea over it, and an octopus therein, having a property of suction. It would suck in a man in armour till he lay at the bottom of its treasure-bag. The Dagda came with his 'mace of wrath' in his hand, and plunged it down upon the octopus, and chanted these words: 'Turn thy hollow head! Turn thy ravening body! Turn thy resorbent forehead! Avaunt! Begone!' Then the magic sea retired with the octopus; and hence, may be, the place was called Mag Muirthemne.* (Gwynn, 1924)

We also see the Dagda in the Dindshenchas of the Brug na Boinde where we are told the story of his affair with Bóinne, wife of Nechtan (alternately Elcmar) who bears Aengus to the Dagda. In this poem the Dagda is called 'red', 'swift', and 'harsh' and we are told that it was the Dagda who built the Brug na Boinde, and that it was here that his son Cermait was born. In the Dindshenchas of Ailech I and Ailech II we are told again that the Dagda was king over the Tuatha Dé Danann, and he is called strong, 'keen', 'active', and 'most famous'. In this place-name story we learn that the Dagda's son Aedh cuckolded another man and was killed in retaliation for it; despite many people calling for the murderer's life, the Dagda decreed that the killer must, instead, build the fort at Ailech as a tribute to Aedh.

In the Dindshenchas of Druim Suamaich, we also learn that there is a place named 'Hill of Tears' for the spot where the Dagda cried over Cermait's death. Gray suggests in her note to the text of the Cath Maige Tuired that the Dagda wept tears of blood over his son (Gray, 1983).

The Dagda in my Life

As we've seen, the Dagda features in many different myths and stories, some more well known than others. My favourite story of the Dagda is the tale of how he obtained his magic staff or club, which I mention above. Of all the stories of the Dagda, this one speaks to me the most and touches me the most deeply.

The image of the Dagda wandering the world, carrying the dead body of his son Cermait, seeking any way to bring his son back to life hits me harder than any image of the Dagda as a king or warrior. This idea of the Great God as a grieving parent looking for some way, any way, to save his child is more beautiful to me than any other. There is also something humorous in visualizing Cermait, brought back to life, looking around and seeing the corpses of the three other men then berating his father, this powerful God who has just carried his corpse over the world, for his lack of fairness in killing the men who provided the means for his own life to be revived.

The Dagda has many stories and there is much wisdom in all of them. But for me this one story, which speaks of a father's love and dedication to his child, is the one that connects most strongly. There is humility in it alongside the awe inspiring divinity that makes me see the Dagda as a God worth honouring.

Endnotes

1. The meaning is uncertain here, however, in context it most likely refers to the three crafting Gods of Goibhniu, Credne and Luchtne.
2. The Morrigan and the Dagda's union at Samhain is an event that I often hear misinformation about so I think it's important to discuss that one specific incident in depth here. Basically, I hear people repeating the idea that the Dagda sought out the Morrigan before Samhain, before a big battle, and had sex with her in exchange for her promise to help fight in the battle and/or for battle advice. This is both an

oversimplification and misinterpretation, I think, of the actual events that transpired. Firstly this meeting is said to be *dia bliadnae* or on a day yearly, which implies that the two meet every year about that time. We are told in other material that the Morrigan is the Dagda's wife, something we discussed in an earlier chapter. So, we see a yearly meeting with two deities who are associated with each other outside of this story as well. The two meet at a pre-arranged location where the Dagda finds the Morrigan straddling a river washing her genitals. The Dagda says something to her – about what, we don't know. After making this union – one may assume having sex, although the word *oentaith* can mean either a physical union or a pact or agreement – the Morrigan tells the Dagda to strip his land, a common military ploy, in the place the Fomorians will be and to gather the armies of the Tuatha Dé Danann, and then promises to go out herself and destroy one of the Fomorian kings with magic, which she subsequently does, bringing back two handfuls of blood as proof. At no point does the story explicitly state that a deal is made between them, or that the Morrigan's actions are in any way a response to or payment for the Dagda's. We can say with certainty that she never makes an offer to him, although we do not know what he says to her when he first sees her.

My personal take on this is simple: The Dagda and the Morrigan meet every year and this particular year their meeting falls just before a major battle. After having sex, the Morrigan tells the Dagda exactly what he is to do and what she herself will be doing until he gathers the armies. Anyone who is married or in a longterm relationship should appreciate the interpersonal dynamics going on here.

Did the Morrigan grant her aid to the Tuatha Dé Danann in trade for the Dagda's attention? There's really no indication of that either in the text. The Morrigan is a member of the Tuatha Dé Danann, daughter of Ernmas and Delbeath according to the Lebor Gabala Erenn, and had every reason to assist the Tuatha Dé Danann without payment. We also need to keep in mind that before this meeting the Morrigan had already gone to Lugh and chanted a battle incitement to encourage him to rise up and fight, so she herself was clearly both in favour of the battle and already encouraging it and acting for the Tuatha Dé Danann.

It's an interesting passage and full of important information about both Gods, but I think we need to be cautious in rushing to interpret it, especially through a modern lens. Instead, I think we need to look at what's actually going on and being said, and what happens, and let the story speak for itself.

3. The Dagda tells the Fomorian princess that he is under a taboo not to carry anyone on his back who doesn't ask him using his name. The Fomorian maiden asks the Dagda his name three times. The first time he says 'Fer Benn', but when she orders him to carry her using that name he replies that it is not his name. The second time he replies that his name is 'Fer Benn Brúach', but again when she asks using this name he says that is not his name. The third time he gives her the much longer name already discussed in the introduction which includes the names he gave at first as well as many more besides. It is likely that there is significance in the question having to be asked three times, and it should be noted that he never actually lies to the maiden; he simply doesn't give her the full answer until the third request.

4. Some people theorize that this encounter is a duplication of the previous one between the Dagda and the Morrigan. I personally believe this is likely a separate event that merely bears some surface similarities. It is true that in several places in the Cath Maige Tuired there are incidents that seem to repeat, such as this scene and both Nuada and Lugh at

different points asking the gathered Gods what powers they will bring to the fight. It is possible that these duplications represent different versions of the story that have been combined into a single narrative. It is also possible that the original story merely had certain repetitive elements to it. That all said, there are enough notable difference between the Dagda's encounter with the Morrigan and the unnamed Fomorian princess to say that the two are at the least different stories rather than literally the same incident repeated. The Morrigan and the Fomorian princess are different personages, and their interactions with the Dagda have very different tones.

5. By many reckonings, Bodb is the Dagda's son and Aengus's half-brother. It is logical that even if he couldn't command Bodb as a king he could ask him as his father.

6. Yes the same Ailill and Medb from the Ulster Cycle. This story is actually one of the pre-tales to the Táin Bó Cuialigne and ends by explaining that Ailill and Medb's help to Aengus is why Aengus sent 3,000 warriors to aid Medb and Ailill during the infamous cattle raid.

Chapter 3

The Dagda's Possessions and Associations

From Murias, a huge great treasure,
the cauldron of The Dagda of lofty deeds.
(MacAlister, 1941, Lebor Gabala Erenn)

Understanding the Dagda's names and connections to other deities is an important beginning to understanding the Dagda's nature. Another key step towards a greater insight to Himself is looking at the items he possesses and which are associated with him. These are all things that reflect his nature in some way and their connection to him also demonstrates their own greater cosmological significance.

He was said to be a master of Druidic magic and to possesses several magical objects. Each of these objects in their own way gives us insight into the Dagda and also a place to connect more fully to him. We can learn about him through his stories of course, and we will be looking at many of those in the next chapter, but we can also learn about him directly by studying the things that he is connected to and what they represent.

Cauldron – It was the Dagda who held the cauldron of abundance brought from Murias, one of the four treasures of the Tuatha Dé Danann. *'6. From Murias was brought the Dagda's cauldron. No company ever went away from it unsatisfied'* (Gray, 1983). It is not at all surprising to me that the Dagda, a God who himself is associated with great appetite and excess, would be the holder of such a cauldron. It is also worth noting that despite the modern neopagan association of the cauldron with feminine or Goddess energy, it is actually most often associated with Gods in Irish and more generally Celtic myth. The Dagda has the cauldron of plenty, Dian Cecht has a cauldron (sometimes called a spring) of healing, and there is even a Welsh story about Bran and Branwen that talks about an Irish king who has a cauldron that can revive the Dead. Additionally, we see the poem attributed to Amerigen 'the Cauldron of Poesy' which describes three cauldrons born in every person. The cauldron itself is clearly a very powerful and widespread symbol in Celtic myth, often associated with health or healing, sometimes with rebirth.

The Dagda's cauldron is one of abundance that satisfies all who take from it, a fitting treasure for one who is called Eochaid Ollathair, the Ample Father. I tend to see it as a representation of the qualities of generosity and hospitality, as well as the ability of a leader or head-of-household to provide for those who look to them for support. When I meditate on the cauldron I see it in the light of a source of these things and try to relate that into my own life. I also often end up contemplating the wider symbolism of the cauldron in Irish myth as a provider of abundance and healing. I also personally use the cauldron as a tool in my practice because I feel the symbolism with it is so strong.

The cauldron is, ultimately, a symbol of abundance and plenty. All those who are served from it leave satisfied and in many ways this is a reflection of or perhaps reflected by the Dagda's own personality. He is a God who brings abundance himself, blessing crops and cows.

Staff – He also owned a great staff or club; it is said that one end of the staff could kill nine men with one blow, while the other could heal (Berresford Ellis, 1987; O hOgain, 2006). The Dagda's staff is one of his defining tools, and like his cauldron, in some ways, it symbolises the Dagda himself.

It is often referred to as a club, but in Irish it is called lorg which can mean a staff, stick, club or cudgel, various sources will translate the name of this item differently and what we choose to call it in English does shape how we picture it. I prefer to call it a staff myself because for me that works best with the idea of it killing with one end and giving life with the other, however, other people may prefer a different name and imagery. According to one description from the Cath Maige Tuired, his staff may be forked and the text describes it as so large it required a wheeled cart and eight men to drag it, and it left a trench that could separate provinces behind in its path. This description is interesting in that it is the only place we see his staff described in any detail, and here it is first called 'gabul gicca rothach', that is a pronged pole on wheels before being identified as the Dagda's staff (lorg).

Like the Dagda himself, his staff has various epithets; it is referred to as adúathmar (terrible) and iarnaidi (iron). In one source it is called 'lorg anfaidh' which is translated as 'mace of wrath', however, it could also be read as 'storm staff' (Martin, 2008).

The Dagda's famous magic staff doesn't actually belong to him – it's only on loan. He obtained it while searching for a cure for his son Cermait who had been killed by Lugh for sleeping with Lugh's wife. He came across three men who were arguing over their inheritance which included a club which could kill at one end and revive at the other. The Dagda asked if he could borrow it and promptly used it to kill all three and revive his son, who shamed him into reviving the three men as well. After that he basically refused to return it, but an agreement was reached that he would permanently borrow it, giving the sun, moon, sea and land as sureties against it.

Harp – The Dagda possesses a harp who some people believe could change the seasons, in part because when the Dagda spoke out to call it to him he called it by its two names and also said 'Come summer! Come winter!' (Gray, 1983). The Irish viewed summer and winter as the two primary seasons, divided by Samhain and Bealtaine, the turning points of the year. One could interpret the invocation of these two seasons in conjunction with the harp being called to the Dagda's hand as symbolic of the harp's ability to influence the seasons or symbolic connection to them; I might suggest that even though this concept has become widely accepted we should be somewhat cautious in seeing it as a certain fact.

This harp, along with the Dagda's harpist, was stolen by the Fomorians after the battle of Maige Tuired and the Dagda, with Lugh and Ogma, had to journey to recover it, supporting its importance. Even though it is a harp it is also deadly and when the Dagda called it off the wall where it had been hung, likely as a war trophy, it killed several Fomorians to reach him. The harp has two names: Daur Dá Bláo and Cóir Cetharchair. Daur Dá Bláu means 'Oak of two meadows', and Cóir Cetharchair likely means 'four-cornered truth' (Gray, 1983).

Herbs, Trees, and Resins – traditionally there are few native herbs that can be said to have a direct association with the Dagda. We don't see any references in older mythology or folklore connecting the Dagda to plants or herbs. In modern terms there are a wide range of herbs people may choose to associate with the Dagda but these will be based in personal gnosis and so will vary from person to person or group to group.

The oak does have strong connections to the Dagda. It is said that splits in the trunk of an oak tree are the mark of the Dagda's axe, and one of the names of the Dagda's famous harp is 'Oak of Two Meadows'.

Although in no way native to Ireland, the Dagda does have some association with frankincense and myrrh. In the story of the Dagda acquiring his magical staff we are told that he used these two resins along with 'many herbs' to preserve his son Cermait's body while he was searching for a way to revive him.

Animals – He possessed a special cow, a *'dark, black-maned, trained, spirited heifer'* who could low and have all the cattle of Ireland follow her (Gray, 1983). This cow plays an important role in the story of the Cath Maige Tuired where the Dagda is given the cow as a reward for building a fort for the king, Bres, and later uses her ability to call all the Irish cattle to recover them from the Fomorians.

In a wider sense, it is worth noting that cows, and magical cows, are something we often see in Irish mythology and are usually owned by important deities. For the Dagda to have a cow that is able to control all other cows is indicative in many ways of the Dagda's own nature as a king and leader.

Locations – The Dagda is associated with Brug na Boind, now called Newgrange, and also with a site in Donegal called Grianan Ailech as well as Leighead Lachtmhaighe in Clare, Cnoc Baine in Tyrone and O Chualann in Wicklow (Smyth, 1988; O hOgain, 2006). In the Taking of the Sidhe, the Dagda's homes are said to be Sidhe Leithet Lachtmaige, Oí Asíd, Cnoc Báine, Brú Ruair and Sid in Broga, itself part of the Brug na Boind complex (Waddell, 2015). By another account, the Dagda's home is at Uisnech, placed there because he is king over the Gods and it was the most central location (Leahy, 1906).

Grainen Ailech was built at the Dagda's direction as a memorial to his son Aedh, and although he gave it to his kinsman, Neit, it does still have some associations with him as his son's grave. In one of the Metrical Dindshenchas for Boind it is said that the Brug was built as a grave marker for the Dagda and his three sons, Aengus, Cermait and Aedh.

It is said that it was the Dagda who delegated each of the sidhe to the Tuatha Dé Danann after their defeat by the Milesians, possibly at Manannan mac Lir's suggestion (O hOgain, 2006). By this account, the Dagda originally lived at Brug na Boind but was tricked out of the site by his son Aengus, however, he does have other connections to the site. His son Cermait was said to be born within sight of Sid in Broga and there is a place there mentioned in the Dindshenchas called the Bed of the Couple, said to belong to the Dagda Donn and his 'great woman'. Whether or not the Brug originally belonged to Elcmar/Nechtan or the Dagda, and whether or not ownership was switched to Aengus, the place continues to have a strong association with the Dagda as well as his sons.

The Dagda also has several connections in other areas. We are told in the Cath Maige Tuired that he has a home 'in Glen Etin in the north' and although we don't know today exactly where this is, we know that it was near the various sites of the battles of Maige Tuired. He was said to meet the Morrigan at the river Unshin, and a likely modern site for this is in Sligo near Heapstown Cairn which is said to be the location of the healing well[1] used by the Tuatha Dé Danann during the fighting. Also said to be near there is the place where the Morrigan and Dagda laid together, called 'the Bed of the Married Couple', although this site, like his home at Glen Etin, is not currently known.

Samhain – He is particularly associated with Samhain, a time when many pivotal things occur in Irish mythology. This is when he was said to unite with the Morrigan; this is also the time that he united with the Fomorian princess, and gained not only herself as his mistress but also her assistance against her own people in the battle. Beyond the meeting of the Morrigan and the Dagda at Samhain, it is at also at Samhain that the Dagda advises his son Aengus to trick Elcmar out of ownership of the Brug na Boind in some versions of the myth. Tangentially, Samhain is when the Dagda's son Aengus meets with and obtains Caer, the woman he has been dreaming of, after the Dagda helps him find out who she is.

Samhain is when Lugh sends the Dagda to spy on the Fomorians and when they offer the Dagda a pit full of porridge. The practice of pouring a mixture of porridge containing meat and fruit into the ground at Samhain was also a folk method of honouring the spirits on this holiday (Sjoestedt, 2000). This is something that I do today on the holiday and I know other people who do this as well, offering the Dagda porridge on Samhain as a way to honour him and as a nod to the mythology.

The Dagda in My Life

One aspect of my own personal practice has been utilizing the four treasures of the Tuatha Dé Danann in ritual. For me, having these items is both a symbolic and metaphysical connection to the actual items in the Otherworld. When I first set out to create this set of ritual tools I found it fairly easy to obtain a sword and stone; and only slightly more challenging to find a spear. The cauldron, however, proved to be quite difficult indeed.

I found many different cauldrons, of course, in all sorts of sizes and shapes and materials. But none of them ever felt quite right. None of them resonated with the energy of the Dagda, with that warm, welcoming feeling of hospitality and abundance that I was looking for blended with the subtle aura of the numinous. As time went by I found myself having to use others that were less acceptable just to have something to use, but I was never totally happy about it.

Over time, I think, I started to assume that I was just not going to find that perfect cauldron, that good enough was going to have to do. And then when I least expected it, I found it, although I didn't realize it at the time. Tucked away in a catalogue of deity statues there was a bronze reproduction of the Gundestrap Cauldron and because it can be very difficult to find tools in bronze, I decided to get it. I liked that it was a museum replica and even though my primary focus is Irish and the cauldron's imagery isn't, I was still drawn to it on an aesthetic level.

When it arrived and I first held it in my hands I knew that, for me, this would be the Dagda's cauldron. It had a weight and a presence to it that I'd never felt before, and there was something about the way this cauldron told a story within its panels that spoke to me of the Dagda. It is obviously not the Dagda's actual cauldron nor do I think that it likely resembles what would have been used by the Iron Age Irish, however, for me it is a strong symbolic representation and a powerful reminder of the Dagda's power.

Endnotes

1. Heapstown Cairn is believed to be the location of the well of Slaine, where Dian Cecht and his children, all the main healing gods of the Tuatha De Danann, worked to cure those injured in the fighting. The well was filled with stones by the Fomorians to prevent its use later in the battle. Heapstown Cairn is one of the oldest and largest Neolithic cairns in Europe.

Chapter 4

Good God of All Skills

There was a wondrous king over the Tuatha Dé in Ireland, Dagán by name [i.e. 'the Dagda']. Great was his power, even over the sons of Mil after they had seized the land.
(Carey, 2003, The Taking of the Sid)

One of the things that make the Dagda somewhat unique among the Irish Gods is that he represents a deity who is skilled in all arts, instead of one who specializes. Although in modern paganism he is known for a few specific things, when we look at the mythology we find that he had a wider set of associations than may be apparent at first. Many of these have already been touched on as we've looked at his names, mythology and associations earlier in the book but it's worth taking time here to discuss some of the specific things that the Dagda relates to, how he relates to them and what those things can mean for us as we seek to connect to him.

I want to preface this section by saying that while it is important to understand the things that the Dagda has the strongest connections to, it is also important to keep in mind his repeated brags of being a God good at all skills wielded by other deities. Whereas most other deities have a few things that they primarily focus on, the Dagda claims to do them all and his mythology supports a wide range of abilities and interests. This chapter is meant to highlight a variety of things that we know he focuses on or has strong connections to but it is in no way meant to imply that these are the extent or limits of his abilities or interests. Of all the deities one might choose to honour, the Dagda is perhaps one of the most willing to respond[1] and most flexible in what he can do.

So, we know the Dagda can and will respond to a person for any need. In fairness this is true of any deity but most also have certain areas that are their purviews, namely, things which they are known, in mythology and history, to focus on or have experience with. Calling on a deity connected to death during the birth of a child isn't necessarily a bad thing but it also means involving an energy that may be counterintuitive to that experience. On the other hand, there are some deities such as the Dagda and also Lugh, who is called 'Ildanach' (many skilled), who are known to have broad or multifaceted associations. These Gods of many skills tend to be more balanced in what they do and so, unlike some other deities which may focus entirely or primarily on very specific types of things gods like the Dagda focus on both a thing and its opposite. He is a god of life but also death, of abundance but also endurance during strife, of kingship but also of the common man. This means that the Dagda is uniquely placed to respond to any need a person might have and feel it necessary to call on a god for.

Life and Death

The Dagda is a god who represents both a giver of life and of death. His staff is perhaps the most literal representation of that, in that it kills at one end and revivifies the dead at the other, but he also represents this energy in other ways. He has some cosmogenic aspects as a creator and shaper of the land who brings life and civilization to the world. In Irish mythology where we have no extant creation myth, we often find, instead, stories of deities who create the world in small pieces by clearing areas and creating plains; the Dagda does this in the Wooing of Etain by creating 12 plains and 12 rivers. In contrast he also has clear associations with battle and death, not only as a warrior, which he clearly is, but also in the story where he bears his son's corpse through the world as well as the stories connecting two locations with him which are Neolithic burial mounds.

Fire, Passion, and Earth

In his article discussing the names of the Dagda, Scott Martin also touches on the nature of this multifaceted God, Describing him as both a god of fire and of the earth. He suggests that fire imagery can be seen in his name 'Ruadh Ro-fessa' as well as his claim of boasting all of the powers wielded by the other Gods which he made immediately after Firgol the Druid promised to rain down fire on the Fomorians (Martin, 2008).

One of the Dagda's names is 'Aedh Alainn', with Aedh literally meaning fire or fiery. The Dagda also has a son named Aedh and the two have several similarities. The Dagda, as I just mentioned, is called Aedh Alainn which O hOgain gives as 'Fiery Lustrous one' but Alain might also be rendered as lovely or fine, echoing the epithet of his son Aedh Caem, Aedh the Fair. The Dagda has an affair with Elcmar's wife, although he doesn't face repercussions for it. His son Aedh is killed by Corrgend for sleeping with Corrgend's wife. We may perhaps say that both the Dagda and his son are related to fire and to the fire of passion.

The one physical description we have of the Dagda may be viewed as sexual and it occurs in-between two overtly sexual passages in mythology. In that story, which was related in the previous chapter on mythology, the Dagda meets the Morrigan and sleeps with her, then goes as a spy among the Fomorians dressed in a way that exposes his penis. While, as has been mentioned, this was not an uncommon style of dress for peasants, there has been some suggestion by scholars that the description of his clothing, the mention of his buttocks being exposed, then of his 'wheeled club' needing eight men to lift it and leaving a deep track behind him, followed immediately by the statement that his penis was exposed and hanging down may have been meant as an allusion between his staff/club and his penis (Williams, 2016). This descriptive scene is then followed by his meeting the Fomorian princess and taking her as his concubine, juxtaposing the possible use of his staff/club as an allusion for his penis between two scenes of sex with powerful magical women.

We see the Dagda often connected to the colour brown or dun, and also to oak trees. His physical descriptions in many cases are very earthy in nature. In the Coir Anmann we are told: *'because the Tuatha Dé Danann adored him, because he was a god of the world to them.'* We should consider, though, that 'dia talmhan' can also be read as god of the earth. And in the Wooing of Etain, we see his son Aengus going to him for help to clear 12 plains and create 12 rivers, associating him with cosmogenic acts. He is also associated with creating the three rivers Síur, Eóir and Berba whose sources burst out of the earth in front of him (Gray, 1983).

Weather and Crops

The Dagda is associated with lightning strikes on trees, which are said to be the marks of his axe; one name for his staff is lorg anfaidh which can be read as staff of storms. Additionally, in the beginning of the Tochmarc Etaine we are told: *'He was also named the Dagda [i.e. good god], for it was he that used to work wonders for them and control the weather and the crops'*. We see this idea of the Dagda influencing crops echoed to some degree in the story of the Taking of the Sidhe where he is the deity who the Milesians must deal with in order to have their crops flourish and their cows give milk. It is clear from these sources that the idea of the Dagda as a god who influenced the weather and by extension the success of the crops was an important one. He was described as a being to whom the other Tuatha Dé Danann looked for these things and also someone who mortals had to treat with in order to obtain prosperity. This is a significant thing because at one point in the Lebor Gabala Erenn, Donn of the Milesians had urged his brothers not to acknowledge the Tuatha Dé Danann as Gods but to stay with the Gods they had honoured before; yet once they are living in Ireland they find that only by acknowledging the Dagda and offering to him – by giving the Tuatha Dé Danann a tithe of milk and grain – will they have a harvest of milk and grain of their own.

Warrior

The Dagda is a champion and renowned warrior and we see him fighting in battles in several of the myths he appears in. In the Cét-Cath Maige Tuired, he is clearly described as a battle leader and warrior, not only leading the Tuatha Dé Danann into battle one day but also fighting against the Fir Bolg champions himself. His fighting is described this way:

> *The Dagda set to breaking the battalions and harrying the hosts and dislodging divisions and forcing them from their positions. Cirb, son of Buan, entered the fray from the east and slaughtered brave men and spirited soldiers. The Dagda heard Cirb's onset, and Cirb heard the Dagda's battering blows. They sprang each at the other. Furious was the fight as the good swords fenced, heroic the heroes as they steadied the infantry, and answered the onslaughts. At last Cirb fell before the Dagda's battering blows.* (Frazer, 1916)

When Nuada is injured, the Dagda is one of two champions said to have rushed to his defence who drove off the attacking Fir Bolg to save the king's life. In the Cath Maige Tuired he fights against the Fomorian Cetlenn, wife of Balor.

At this point we don't have much information about the Dagda in this role: we don't know what he would have been wearing, although we do know as is referenced in the quote above that he fought with a sword, but we can safely assume, I think, that his equipment would have been standard for the time period. The social order of early Ireland was complex and highly structured, and from this we know that being a warrior and champion had a special significance and rank. For the Dagda to have this role within Nuada's kingship when the Tuatha Dé Danann first arrived in Ireland would have bestowed a level of prestige.

Poet and musician

In the Cét-Cath Maige Tuired we see the Dagda taking on the role of poet, which in pagan Ireland was more involved and complex than what people today might envision. A poet not only composed poetry and songs but also retold great events and was the historian for a king. It is this role that we see the Dagda performing, as Nuada asks him to relate the events of that day's battle and the Dagda responds with a poetic retelling of the battle: who had fought who, who had fallen, and who had been victorious.

He was also a musician as we see in the Cath Maige Tuired where he plays his harp for the Fomorians, and uses all three types of music that musicians were renowned for. He plays the sorrowful music, the joyful music and finally, the sleep music, showing that he has mastered all of them.

King

The Book of Lecan states that the Dagda ruled for 80 years as king of the Gods after the death of Lugh, but other sources state that he was killed fighting Cetlenn at the second battle of Maige Turied (Smyth, 1988). This is later explained with a story saying that he took a wound in the battle that took 80 years to kill him,[2] but that is clearly an attempt to unify the varying tales into a coherent whole (O hOgain, 2006). In several stories, the Dagda is called the king of the fairy mounds of Ireland and it's implied he has authority over all the fairy hills and their rulers.

The Dagda's central position and importance as a ruler may be reinforced by a reference from the Tochmarc Etaine which says that his home was at Uisnech because it was 'in the centre of Ireland ... Ireland stretching equally far from it on every side, south and north, to east and west' (Leahy, 1906). He is called 'a just-Dealing lord over the feast' and 'king of Erin with hosts of hostages' and the Dindshenchas says: 'Who was king over all Erin, sweet-sounding, radiant? Who but the skilful Dagda? You hear of none other *so famous'* (Gwyn, 1924).

Of all the Gods who take on the role of King of the Tuatha De Danann, and there are many, the Dagda seems to have been one of the best and most effective and had the longest rule. Nuada rules for 27 years (not-contiguously), Lugh ruled for 40 years, the Dagda for 80, Delbeath for 10, Fiacha for 10, then the Dagda's grandsons MacCecht, McGreine, and MacColl ruled together for 29 until the Milesians arrived. Although the Tuatha De Danann are driven into the fairy mounds after this point, at least one source tells us that the Dagda is king over the Gods again: *'There was a marvellous king of the Tuatha Dea in Ireland. Dagda was his name. Great was his power, even in the present time when the Sons of Mil have taken the land'* (Daimler, 2015).

The Dagda reinforces this idea of his true kingship in the Dindshenchas when his son Aedh's killer is brought before him; the people are crying for his death in retribution and the Dagda responds:

> *'I will not do as ye say', said the Dagda: 'that which is not right and lawful may not be done by me.'*
>
> *'Life and honour are not due as the price of a life: this shall not turn aside the Dagda's face from the divine decree.'* (Gwynn, 1924)

The idea that kingship in Ireland rested in true justice is one that is deeply embedded in the culture – a good king upholds truth and gives true judgements and by these actions his people and land flourish. In contrast, a bad king does not uphold the truth and gives false judgements which undermine the success and security of his people. This concept is called fír flatha (prince's truth) and this idea of justice versus injustice is an aspect of what destroys the kingship of Bres who acts against truth when he renders a false judgement against the Dagda in the case of Cridenbel's death (O Cathasaigh, 2014). In contrast to Bres's bad rule and injustice we have the example of the Dagda's good rule and refusal to act against justice even when his own interests would benefit. This relationship to truth is reflected by the king's relationship to the goddess of sovereignty who chooses him as ruler and blesses his reign as long as he rules well, but who acts to remove him with the help of Otherworldly forces when he rules badly.

Sage and Magician

Several of the Dagda's names refer to his great wisdom or skill and we see this power in action in some of his stories. The Coir Anmann tells us: '*Ruadh Rofesa that is it was he who had the wholeness of heathen knowledge*'; heathen knowledge being synonymous with occult or magical knowledge here. We also see the Dagda in the Cath Maige Tuired promising to wield all the magical powers that the sorcerers and druids are promising to use as well as later swearing that he will smite the Fomorians with 'destruction and wizardry'. The specific word used that Gray translates as wizardry here is 'amaidichtai' a form of ammaitecht which means witchcraft and, interestingly, is usually connected explicitly to women. The word given for destruction is admilliud which does mean destruction but also means injuring by magic or casting the evil eye; this is the exact same word the Morrigan uses when promising to attack the Fomorian King, Indech. We may perhaps argue that in this scene from the Cath Maige Tuired, the Dagda is in fact promising to fight for the men of Ireland with mutual cutting (cáemslecht), injurious magic and witchcraft.

I would like to note here that although the Dagda does have a strong modern reputation as a Druid or worker of druidic magic there is nothing explicit in mythology that connects him to this. One might argue that his connections to poetry, wisdom and magic working creates an indirect association with Druidry and I won't argue for or against that. I will point out that we are told in the Metrical Dindshenchas that the Dagda had his own druid[3] which seems a bit redundant if he was a druid himself, but the reader is free to draw their own conclusions.

Although not directly related to Druidism, the Dagda does have some connections to blacksmiths although these are now obscure and difficult to understand. We see this in references from the Irish triads and Law Tracts which state that there are three things which give status to a blacksmith and these are: *'the cooking-spit of Nethin, the cooking-pit of the Morrigan, and the anvil of the Dagda'* (Kelly, 1988). What exactly the anvil of the Dagda was, though, is uncertain.

Farmers and Workers

In many ways the Dagda is a God of the common man, even though he is – from the mythology – one of the best kings among the Tuatha Dé Danann. Although I would hesitate to say he is a direct cognate to Gods from other pantheons, as he is clearly himself with his own unique mythology and personality, it can certainly be said that he has much in common with the Norse Thor: both have associations with striking weapons, with storms, with fertility of crops and with great wisdom. The Dagda as a God of crops and weather was naturally enough a deity of farmers, a connection we see often among other pantheons. We also see the Dagda acting directly to shape the earth as in the story from the Cath Maige Tuired where he builds the fort for Bres, labouring in the earth to achieve the task.

The description of his attire when he goes to the Fomorians in the Cath Maige Tuired is also the dress of the common man not a noble. Whereas people of his station would wear long tunics and fine boots the Dagda is described in a very short – even obscenely short – tunic, with rough hide shoes; Sjoestedt points out that this is *'The attire of ordinary churls'* (Sjoestedt, 2000, p. 39). After leaving the Fomorian camp, the Dagda is described as being naked from the waist down with his genitals exposed, something a modern audience may find shocking but was actually standard attire for peasantry of the time (Williams, 2016). While we might look on this now and see it as comedic or even as a revisionist attempt to lessen the esteem of the Dagda, we may perhaps also argue that this appearance directly connects the god to the common man, showing him dressed and acting as the common people did rather than as nobility.

Grieving Parent

Certainly not a skill, by most measures, but nonetheless a theme we see associated with the Dagda that deserves consideration here. The Dagda, as has been mentioned, was the parent of many children and through them connected to grieving. His daughter Brighid invented the concept of keening when she mourned her son Rúadan (the Dagda's grandson) who died during the battle of Mag Tuired.[4] Three of the Dagda's sons are killed and we know that at least two of them are mourned by him in ways that echo each other. When Cermait dies, the Dagda carries his body around the world after preserving it with resins and herbs, searching for a way to bring life back to his son. When Aedh is killed the Dagda, who is king at the time, commands the murderer to carry Aedh's body on his back from Tara looking for a memorial stone that matched it; this was found near Lough Foyle and then the guilty man had to carry both the body and stone to Ailech in Donegal where Aedh's grave was built (MacNeil, 1962).

The Dagda in My Life

I was 11 when I first became interested in paganism and 12 when I committed to a witchcraft path, based on a popular public form of Wicca found in easily available books. Based on my initial understanding of how that whole thing was supposed to work and a limited knowledge of Irish mythology, my pre-teen self decided that I was required to choose a god and a goddess to honour, and the first god I ever worshipped in a formal ritual was the Dagda. I look back on it now and cringe a bit to think of my young self and my nascent approach to religion, but I have fond memories of the Dagda.

As a child connecting for the first time to named pagan Gods, I am glad in retrospect that the Dagda was one of the first I reached out to. Although I know that I wasn't using the best information, I was sincere in my efforts and of all the deities I could have reached out to, the Dagda is, in my experience, one of the kindest and most gentle particularly with children. I might cringe at my ignorance but I always felt his presence as welcoming and protective, which was something I particularly appreciated at that point in my life.

When I first reached out to the Dagda I was only a child and my understanding of him was a child's understanding shaped by, what I won't deny were, very poor sources. To me he was a divine father figure, large and jovial and endlessly giving. It took me many, many years to see the other layers to him, to understand that he was a complex figure who could be simultaneously the common fort-builder and the regal king, the powerful Druid and the father advised by his own son, the passionate God and the earth shaper.

I think that one of the most amazing things about this multifaceted deity is the way that he can connect with so very many people across the range of human experiences. Many gods are relatable but the Dagda has stories that speak to direct experiences of suffering in ways that are painfully human. His stories encompass our own lives, from suffering to triumph, from oppression to celebration. He lusts for what he cannot have and cuckolds another man to get what he wants; this speaks to me of the envy and jealousy I think we all feel sometimes for what others have and we want. He loses two of his sons when they also act on their passions, and a third son for seeking to marry a woman he can't have; this speaks to me of the grief we all go through in life when we lose loved ones in ways that seem to us senseless or avoidable. He is set to digging and building a fort by an unjust ruler and at the same time is in a position where his sustenance is taken from him unfairly by a satirist; I think we can all empathise with such situations where we are forced by circumstances to do unpleasant or difficult things we don't want to do. There is something, for me, that makes it especially touching to know that the God of abundance and plenty, who bears a treasure that feeds all who come to it, has known what it is to be hungry.

As I grew older and read more and created a more genuine connection to the Dagda, beyond that child's notion of him as the pre-requisite father, that was when I truly came to understand why he was so popular. Seeing him for more than that surface image of the lusty god of abundance showed me a deity of the entire human experience, and that let me understand why he held such a premiere position in so many myths and for so many people.

Endnotes

1. As has been touched on previously, there is some supposition that the Dagda's epithet of 'swift' related to the speed with which he was believed to respond to the prayers of his followers. We see a similar thing with Dian Cecht and it does seem likely that these deities who were immensely popular in mythology and folk tradition were believed to be very responsive to those who worshipped them.

2. Death among the Gods is always a tricky subject and this is certainly true when we look at the Dagda's alleged death. According to the stories, the Dagda rules as king for 80 years and then dies; yet we have later stories and folklore from the time after humans have come to Ireland that make it clear that the Dagda is still present and to all appearances alive. Similarly we see other stories where a deity is killed and re-appears alive again, sometimes within a short period of time within the same story. In the Cét-Cath Maige Tuired,

Aengaba is killed fighting a Fir Bolg champion one day and yet later goes with the Dagda to aid Nuada after his arm is severed. In the Cath Maige Tuired, Miach is killed by Dian Cecht for healing Nuada's arm, yet shortly thereafter, we are told that the two along with other healing Gods are at the well of healing working on the Tuatha Dé Danann wounded. From this we may perhaps conclude that death to a God is at best an impermanent state.

3. Metrical Dindshenchas poem 24 Ailech III:

Said the Dagda himself, pure of countenance: 'From the stone shall be the place's name' (a saying in its homes).
'Ailech shall this place be called throughout Banba, honoured above hills like the silent hill of Tara,' said the Dagda's druid.

We also know there were a variety of members of the Tuatha Dé Danann who are explicitly listed as or described as Druids in the stories, such as Fingal. Most commonly we see these Druids attached to other named deities, usually deities who are kings or lords, reinforcing the social order of Ireland at the time.

4. The story of Rúadan was not mentioned previously but in brief, he is the son of Brighid and the king, Bres. During the battle of Maige Tuired he goes to spy on the Tuatha De Danann for his father's people, the Fomorians, and while he is there he tries to kill the divine smith, Goibniu. He does this by casting one of Goibniu's own spears at him. This attempt fails, however, and Goibhniu pulls the weapon out of his own wound and casts it back at Rúadan, killing him.

Chapter 5

The Dagda in the Modern World

The Dagda sat with his back to an oak tree. He looked like a workman, and his hands were as hard as the hands of a mason, but his hair was braided like the hair of a king. He had on a green cloak with nine capes, and along the border of every cape there was a running pattern embroidered in gold and silver and purple thread. (Young, 1910, Celtic Wonder Tales)

We have already looked at the Dagda's role in the older mythology but his existence is not static; he continues to appear in newer mythology and even modern fiction and video games. It is important to understand his roles here as well as they also shape how people today understand him as a god. While I might argue that there is great value in the older myths and material that needs to be considered and remembered, we must also keep in mind that belief and folklore are ever evolving things. The Dagda is as much a god of today's world as he was a god of the Iron Age world, and he remains as relevant and important today as ever.

In modern terms, the Dagda is often associated with leadership, wisdom, strength, abundance, fertility, generosity and Druidic magic. His association with Druids and Druidic magic is one that tends to get a lot of attention by some modern authors, especially – and unsurprisingly – among modern Druids. Author Ian Corrigan of Ar nDraiocht Fein, America's largest neo-druid group, goes so far as to say that the Dagda's *'key function is as Druid of the Gods'* (Corrigan, 2017).

Although I dislike the way that some authors describe him as the God of the Druids since I feel that this is an overly narrow view, there is certainly merit in this as he does have connection to magic if not the more overtly priestly functions of the Druids. I think if we did want to follow this perspective we could tentatively suggest a symbolic connection between his staff and the Druidic staff or wand. People who choose to see him this way at the least have one hundred years or more of precedent to look to.

Another modern view that is extremely pervasive is that of the Dagda as a sun/solar God. This is is rooted in both academia as well as the tendency during the eighteenth and nineteenth centuries to view all Gods through a mould fashioned from Classical Greek and Roman deities. This view is one that does not tend to mesh well with the Irish deities who rarely can be shoehorned into Classical frameworks successfully, however, because of the popularity of this approach even among scholars it is a pervasive and widespread view. Through this lens the Dagda with his many fire associations is naturally labelled a solar God and many books will repeat this idea as a fact without arguing to support it. As with seeing the Dagda as a god of Druids, while there may not be a precedent in mythology there is certainly a modern precedent at this point of people seeing the Dagda as a sun god for over a century now.

The Dagda in Modern Myths

We can't really discuss the Dagda in the modern world without looking at how he has appeared in some of the more creative retellings of the myths, those that take the most liberties with the mythology. Although these can often vary greatly from the actual stories we recapped in a previous chapter, they nonetheless strongly influence modern pagan views and understandings of the Dagda.

Lady Gregory was a contemporary of William Butler Yeats and did much to record the folktales and myths she came across in Ireland. While her intentions may well have been good and her work has certainly been very popular and served as a basis for many other people's understanding of Irish mythology, she did take a considerable amount of creative liberty in her writing. In places, this makes the story she is telling more evocative and engaging, however, it also at times adds material or changes a story in ways that alter it considerably from the source material. It's important to keep this in mind when reading her work.

Ella Young was a visionary and poet in the late nineteenth and early twentieth centuries. She wrote a very poetic version of the myths in 1910, called 'Celtic Wonder Tales' which sought to retell some of the major myths and in some cases to imagine myths that we do not have, such as a creation story. Although very evocative and much loved by people, her versions wandered far from the older myths and were closer to modern fiction that actual mythology. In her version, Brighid is the driving force in the creation of the earth and its life, and she is the one who convinces the Tuatha Dé Danann to go there. Young calls the Dagda by terms such as 'Shepherd of the Star Flocks' and 'Green Harper'. By her account, when the Fomorians put the Tuatha Dé Danann under tribute they took his cauldron and harp from him. He recovered the harp in her story after he and Aengus were captured by the Fomorians and taken with Balor's son to Balor's hall during a feast; then the Dagda called the harp to him and played it, striking the Fomorians speechless and immobile. His playing created life and beauty in the land the Fomorians had laid waste to before he and Aengus fled. The cauldron couldn't be retrieved until Lugh came and the Gods finally rose up and fought against the Fomorians, although this happens very differently in Young's version of the story.

Peter Berresford Ellis is an author with a background in journalism and Celtic studies. He has written a variety of titles on topics relating to Celtic paganism over the years, many of which mention the Dagda. Some of these works are more academic in nature while others are less so; it is often difficult for readers to distinguish between the two. In his book *Celtic Myths and Legends* he offers retellings of myths from different Celtic cultures including the Irish and attempts to offer his version of a creation myth. In this story the world begins with Danu and Bile, a primordial river and tree respectively. The tree produces two acorns which contain the Dagda and Brighid. These two in turn unite to create all of the rest of the world.

Fictional Depictions

The Dagda was once one of the most popular of the Irish Gods, appearing in a variety of myths and he left his mark on the landscape of Ireland with his association with many place names. Outside of paganism he can also be found today in some unexpected places although he often bears little resemblance to the Good God of Ireland. The following is by no means an exhaustive list but represents a small sampling of things in which I am aware of the Dagda's appearance.

The Dagda appears as a character in Pat O'Shae's *Hounds of the Morrigan*. When the Morrigan finds out that she can regain her power by recovering a stone that has a drop of her blood on it, the Dagda enlists two children to go on a quest to stop her, with the aid of his own (adult) children Bridget and Aengus in disguise.

Juliet Marillier's second book of her 'Sevenwaters' series includes a character retelling the story of the Dagda helping Aengus find Caer.

In the recent television show 'Shannara', based on a series of books by Terry Brooks, the Dagda Mor is featured as the ultimate enemy of the civilized peoples of the world. This fiction turns the Dagda from a deity into an elf who was warped by a desire for power and sought to rule the world by controlling a horde of demons. He was imprisoned and in the show is working to escape and try again to take power.

Marvel Comics featured a character named Dagda, also called Eochaid Ollathir, who was king of the Tuatha Dé Danaan.[1]

In what I may describe as typical Marvel fashion, the storyline gets some aspects of the Dagda's mythology correct while other aspects of the mythology are entirely inaccurate.

The Dagda features in the video game Shin Megami Tensei IV: Apocalypse. In the game, which is set in a dystopian future, the Dagda is a deity who brings the player's character back to life and gives them their mission.

The Dagda is also a gaming character in Trinity: Souls of Zill O'll.

'The Iron Druid' series makes references to the Dagda, usually unflattering ones.

Re-envisioning an Iron Age God

When we read about descriptions of the Dagda in mythology we are given an image of a large, robust man; sometimes dressed comically in a short tunic that exposes his genitals and buttocks; sometimes as a king and warrior; sometimes as a common labourer. There are no surviving Iron Age depictions of the Dagda in stone or artwork and modern depictions of him in art tend to favour an anachronistic view picturing him in tunic and trews, often as an older man. He is imagined as he is described in the stories, in all those many iterations. We live in a modern world that speaks a different symbolic language than the Irish of 2,000 years ago, yet we still look at the Dagda through that older lens.

I think what we forget is that the images we base our ideas of the Gods on were not archaic when they were made. As far as I have been able to tell through my own research, the images of deities in ancient art largely feature depictions of contemporary fashion. When we see descriptions of people coming out of the sidhe, the fairy hills, in the Irish myths, they are always said to be wearing fine clothing that seems to be of the same fashion as the people in the stories. When we read them now they seem archaic to us but to people telling the stories they weren't, they were often describing what for them was contemporary fashion.

So, if we know that the depictions of the Gods that we are familiar with actually represent what were at the time modern fashion, why do we as modern Pagans/Polytheists so consistently depict our deities in historic fashions?

Talking to friends, it seems that part of it is just habit. We are used to visualizing them in a certain way, so, when we see them in modern guises some people find it off putting. For other people, the idea of the Gods as anything but archaically dressed is almost sacrilegious in itself. One friend even went so far as to say that he felt seeing the Gods in modern attire made them feel less divine somehow, and made it harder for him to connect to them as deities. I'd like to gently suggest, though, that the idea of modern depictions of the Gods represents a natural way to view them, for people who do choose to see their Gods this way. Visualizing the Gods in modern attire anchors them firmly in our world, in our reality, and can make them more relatable.

There is a certain logic to it; those of us who see the Gods adapting and evolving to the modern world see them appearing in more modern ways. After all we live in a modern world and most people will agree that the Gods have adapted to it, even if we haven't yet agreed on which God to pray to for, say, the internet or internal combustion engines. But do we picture the God we pray to for safety during surgery wearing a tunic from two thousand years ago or wearing modern doctor's clothing? Do we see the Goddess we are offering to for success in a modern business venture wearing a leine and brat or wearing a business suit? Neither option is right or wrong, but it seems like the archaic clothing is the default when the modern clothing is actually closer to what our ancestors would have understood and expected in their own contexts.

We live in a thoroughly modern world, and the gods are as much a part of our world now as they have ever been. Obviously, how I envision each of the deities I honour is based on how I personally relate to them and what I associate them with. If you're comfortable seeing your Gods in ancient dress that's fine and I'm not trying to criticize that, but it's interesting to consider the alternative. How would your Gods dress if they were clothed in modern times?

How would you see the Dagda if you imagined him appearing today? As a king or leader, I could see him wearing a business suit. As a labourer, perhaps he might wear study work boots, jeans and a work shirt. How would you envision him as a modern magic worker? As a musician playing his harp? As a warrior?

I think it's valuable as we discuss the Dagda in the modern world to truly see him in this modern context, to see him as a living force with us today instead of as a snapshot from history. He is a god of abundance and plenty, would modern grocery stores fall under his purview now? As a god of wisdom and knowledge, can we pray to him for help with computer issues? I think these are invaluable questions for all of us to be asking as we seek to connect to the Dagda and to relate to him in a suburban or urban setting.

Altars and Offerings

Building an altar or small shrine for the Dagda is a great way to begin connecting to him and there are many ways to approach this. There is a good amount of artwork that represents the Dagda and it ranges widely in style and perspective. Much of it tends to rely on the description of the Dagda from the Cath Maige Tuired, although there are other pieces, such as those by Jim Fitzpatrick or Jane Brideson which depict him differently. It is very difficult to find statues of the Dagda, however, and usually you will have to either commission a special piece or consider modifying an existing statue that represents a different deity to work for your purpose. The other option is not to use any literal imagery but only use symbolic images or representations, such as a staff or club on your altar to represent the Dagda's presence.

Because he is a God of so many skills and who encompasses so many attributes, you have more freedom to be creative in what you place on his altar than you might with a deity who has more specific symbols. I might suggest beginning by looking at what particular energy relating to the Dagda you may want to draw into your life or nurture a connection with. Below I am going to include a selection of possibilities just to give people some starting points but as always keep in mind that these are meant to be ideas for you to use as a springboard, not rigid plans to follow exactly.

To connect to the Dagda as poet or musician perhaps make a space and include a small replica of a harp with imagery connected to summer and winter. Since poetic inspiration (imbas) among the Irish was sometimes described as a fire in the head, taking a line from a poem by Amergin Glúingel, you might include a candle you could light to represent inspiration. This would also nicely symbolise the Dagda's connection to fire.

To connect to the Dagda as god of the earth and its abundance perhaps drape a brown or tan cloth over a table or shelf and place a bowl of soil on it. You could place stones around that or use stones to build a cairn on the soil if you prefer.

To connect to the Dagda as king of the Tuatha Dé Danann or as a warrior perhaps use purple, blue or red. You might place a sword – either real or a smaller replica – there along with any imagery that speaks to you of Iron Age Irish warriors.

To connect to the Dagda as a magic worker perhaps use a white cloth and bowls holding earth, water and fire which are three specific elements that the Dagda manipulates magically in the stories. This imagery could also be used to represent the Dagda as a creator/cosmogenic God.

To connect to the Dagda as a giver of abundance and prosperity consider placing a replica of his cauldron in an appropriate space.

Offerings for the Dagda, like altar imagery, can be diverse.

When I honour the Dagda I prefer to offer dark beers or ales, and I have also recreated a version of the porridge described as his in the Cath Maige Tuired (although in a much smaller quantity). On Samhain each year I try to offer him this porridge either left out in a bowl or poured into the earth. Since he was the god who the Milesians made a pact with about sharing their harvest you could also choose to offer him milk and grain, which coincidentally enough is what is in porridge. I have also found him very receptive to being offered a portion of any meal I myself am having.

The Dagda is a god of action so beyond giving him the food and drink offerings mentioned above you can also choose to give him intangible things. Write him songs or poems or tell stories in his honour. Work the earth, build new things that benefit others or grow food from the soil that will feed others (whether those others are your family and friends or local wildlife). Act to defend those in your community who are defenceless or do what you can to uphold truth in the world.

Prayers and Invocations

One essential way to connect to any deity in modern times is through praying to them however you view that working for you, and by invoking them in a ritual context. To that end I am going to offer a variety of prayers and invocations for the Dagda in this section. These are meant to be used, of course, but they can also serve as a jumping off point for you to write your own material as well.

Invocation to the Dagda

Red God of Great Knowledge,
Horse Lord, Ample Father,
God who is good at all things,
Dagda, I call to you.

Invocation to the Dagda 2

Dagda, king of the Tuatha De Danann,
Wise Lord, Master of Magic,
Dagda, giver of abundance,
Keeper of the cauldron,
Speaker of true justice,
Dagda, I call to you,
I invoke you,
I invite you to this space.

Prayer to the Dagda for Eloquence

Dagda, who was master of harp and song,
Help me now to find my own voice,
Help me to speak well and with skill,
Help me to find the right words,
Dagda, teller of great tales and mighty deeds,
Let me succeed in telling my own tale,
Let me achieve my own mighty deed,
Let me speak well and truly,
Dagda, let it be so.

Prayer to the Dagda When Grieving a Child

Dagda, ample father, parent to many children,
You who had many fine sons and daughters,
You who buried your son Aedh beneath Ailech,
You who wept tears of blood for your son Cermait,
You who lost Conan to another man's fear,
My own grief consumes me now,
May I find your strength in my suffering,
May I find your courage in my darkness,
May I find your persistence in my grief.

The Dagda in My Life

I don't think I ever really understood what it was to connect to the Dagda when I was honouring him by myself. That isn't in any way to say that I wasn't successful or didn't feel like I had established a genuine connection to him when I was practising my religion alone, because I did. As I've already mentioned, I began honouring him when I was very young and I certainly felt like he was there and not only that but there with me during some very challenging times in my life. But it wasn't until I met other people who honoured the Dagda, and more than that for whom honouring him was a primary focus, that I really understood who the Dagda was. It wasn't until I saw that reflection of Himself in another human being that I truly understood, on a deep spiritual level, things that had previously only been mental exercises.

I've given that a lot of thought in the intervening time and I think that ultimately it is because the Dagda is a God of community and of social groups. Everything that he does and is centres on these concepts and while we can understand that by ourselves, we simply cannot experience that until we share a mutual respect and honour him with other people. When we look at all of the many things that he is associated with and which he does most often, those things come back to supporting his tuath, his people, or creating support for a community. This is true whether we are looking at his clearing plains and creating rivers, building a fort – or ordering one built – distributing homes to the Gods, utilizing his cauldron to ensure no one who comes to it leaves unsatisfied, or even his actions spying on the Fomorians for his side during a war, which ultimately gained him and the Tuatha Dé Danann a valuable ally in Indech's daughter.

He is a God of society, building and maintaining, and this is so intrinsic to his nature that it is a core part of who he is. To understand the Dagda is to see that unspoken connection that holds a community together and to realize that that connection is an aspect of the Dagda as much as anything else that can easily be put into words and added to a compendium.

I realized this when I saw people connected to the Dagda together in a communal setting. But I truly understood it when I was part of a group, including a priest of the Dagda, at Ogulla holy well in Tulsk, County Roscommon. We were visiting the well and hearing about its history and possible connections to some pagan Druidesses, but as part of the visit our guide asked that each of us in the group help clean the well of some waterweeds choking it. We were only required to pull a handful each, but instead we all, as a group, cleaned the entire well not only of the weeds but also pulling out sundry trash that had gone into it over time. Each person had different abilities and comfort levels with the work and yet without any intention or pre-arranged plan we all simply began doing the work. As a group we each did what our skills permitted, what we could do and were comfortable doing, until the well was clean and free flowing.

And looking around after that at the work that was accomplished and at the faces of the other people, I found that I understood the Dagda much better than I ever had before.

Endnotes

1. The correct spelling is Tuatha Dé Danann, however, during the Victorian period the mis-spelling of Danaan became common and was carried forward. It can be found now in a variety of places including books. It is not consistent with any form of Irish spelling, though, and should be viewed as entirely spurious and without meaning.

Conclusion

The Dagda is a difficult God to summarize although he seems like he should be an easy enough deity to describe. He is good at all things, as he himself claims, earning his name of 'Good God' and yet we have seen that within that range of all things there are certain specific ones that he does seem to specialize in. Those things that touch on human endeavours and needs, for example, are his special purviews: weather, crops, abundance, building, battle, working the earth, life, death, wisdom, magic and music. He is a king, immense and majestic, and yet he is described in terms befitting a common worker and his enemies mock his abundant appetites. And his appetites are certainly earthy and abundant, as he himself is.

He is a god of fire and all the goodness that comes with fire, yet we see in him none of the temper that is often associated with fire deities; like his daughter Brighid, he is a deity of compromise and community building rather than burning to the ground. When his son is killed by Lugh he seeks a way to revivify his child, not destroy Lugh – in contrast, when Lugh's father is killed by the sons of Tuireann, Lugh does everything in his power to ensure that they do not survive the compensation he asks of them. When his son Aedh is killed, he is the voice of reason stilling the cries for the murderer's death and instead dealing out a fit punishment that is a King's justice. He is fiery and passionate, and certainly not immoderate in his passions, yet he is also just and compassionate in many stories.

He is a god of the earth and the blessings of the earth and yet nothing in him shies away from the crudeness of the earth that many others stand above. He is a deity who copulates in fields, who relieves himself in ditches, who drags his staff behind him leaving a deep trench in his wake. He unabashedly carries a princess on his back and then takes her as his lover, turning her against her own people and gaining an advantage for his own side at the same time. He builds in the earth and we can picture him as a God with dirt beneath his fingernails, and yet he is also a harpist and poet who relates great events to a king.

Williams may say it best in *Ireland's Immortals* when he describes the Dagda as *'wry, brave, earthy, full of appetite, endearingly long suffering'* (Williams, 2016, p. 125). He is the most empathetically mortal of divine beings, and his stories resonate with us still today because they speak to a greater truth of the human experience albeit played out on a divine stage. There is something somewhere in one of the Dagda's many tales that connects to each of us in some way, I think, as we move through life and deal with our struggles and successes. And there is something deeply powerful in that.

This book is by its very nature as a Pagan Portal only a small taste of the material associated with the Dagda. I strongly encourage anyone who has read this and is interested in learning more to begin by reading the original myths for themselves, preferably several different versions and translations. I would also suggest that people continue looking for and asking for more material to be written about the Dagda because only such a demand will eventually produce full-length books focused on him.

There are many Gods who are active in the world today or who are becoming more active. We see them discussed often on social media, written about in books, depicted in artwork. They are the popular Gods and often they are ones who are connected to things that are flashy which people are drawn to. The Morrigan and Brighid are very well known among Irish Goddesses, and Lugh is probably the god I hear named the most often. People gravitate to them because they are well known and because they represent things that people want to connect to on different levels. The Dagda has his fame as well, but his dedicated followers are not as flashy or as outspoken – so far

– as those of other deities. And yet the Dagda, in many ways, is exactly the deity that the world most needs right now. A god who is a good and just king, a powerful warrior and wielder of magic but also a generous provider; a deity who knows what it means to work hard to build. He is a God of kings and the common person, who can relate to human beings on many levels and in many situations. He is a God who is present and waiting for more of us to hear him and listen to what he is saying.

His cauldron is always ready to serve those who are welcomed before it – and none will go away from it unsatisfied.

Appendix A – Resources

Beyond the books recommended in the bibliography, I would also suggest that people might find value in these resources as well:

Scealai Beag – a wonderful resource for modern storytelling focused on the Dagda. https://harpandclub.blogspot.com

Mary Jones's Celtic Collective is a great resource in general and has both good Dagda information as well as a collection of many of the pertinent texts that mention him. http://www.maryjones.us/ctexts/inDex_irish.html

Another good resource for the original source material is the Corpus of Electronic Texts, or CELT, online. Hosted by the University College Cork, the site offers a variety of material in different languages. https://celt.ucc.ie/publishd.html

The Dublin Institute of Advanced Studies has a website that offers a selection of print material here https://books.dias.ie/ and I also highly recommend The Irish Texts Society as a resource for printed material as they offer dual language books and texts in the original Irish. http://irishtextssociety.org/ . Another good resource for print material is the academic publisher Four Courts Press http://www.fourcourtspress.ie/

John Waddell offers a series of lectures that can be found on youTube now which, in part, discuss the Dagda and are worth watching although he does favour the idea of the Dagda as a sun god:

Confronting Ancient Myth https://www.youtube.com/watch?v=kIgmrnc3zyQ

The Otherworld Hall on the Boyne https://www.youtube.com/watch?v=uzAcx8kr6SM

In Pursuit of the Otherworld https://www.youtube.com/watch?v=-GI98d0EdAg

The Horse Goddess https://www.youtube.com/watch?v=8Yq FMGxGcFo

The Goddess of Sovereignty https://www.youtube.com/watch?v=wtybVh7KCq4

Sacral Kingship https://www.youtube.com/watch?v=f-GlSEP8Us8

Appendix B – Pronunciation Guide

For those who don't have any Irish, pronouncing the names of the different Irish deities and items from mythology can sometimes be confusing. Hopefully this basic guide will be of some help. Pronunciation isn't straightforward and please keep in mind that there will always be regional variations. I am going to offer both the Older Irish and Modern Irish; again just keep in mind that they are different. Old Irish (more properly old/middle/ early modern Irish) is to Modern Irish what Middle English is to Modern English, that is, they bear a resemblance to each other but they don't necessarily sound the same.

Older Irish
Aedh – 'AY-th' with the 'th' like in thing
Aengus – 'AYN-guhs'
Áine – 'AWN-yuh'
Badb – BAY-thv
Brig – BREEG
Caer – KAYR
Cermait – KEHR-myat
In Dagda – ehn DAHG-dah
Danu – DAHN-oo
Dian Cecht – DEEN keht
Finnbheara – FIN-vay-rah
Goibniu – GOV-nih-oo
Macha – MAHK-ah
Morrigan – MORE-rihg-ahn
Nemain – NEHV-ahn

Modern Irish
Aedh – 'AY'
Aengus – 'AN-gus'

Áine – 'AWN-yuh'
Badb – BAY-v or BOW
Brighid – BREED or VREED
Caer – Kare
Cermait – KEHR-mate
An Daghda – ahn DAY(g)-duh
Danu – DAH-noo
Dian Cecht – DEEahn ceht
Finnbheara – FIN-vahra
Goibhniu – GOYV-noo (with the oy like in boy)
Macha – MAHK-ah
Morrigan – MORE-ree-han
Nemain – NEHV-ane

Bibliography

Black, G., (1894) *Scottish Charms and Amulets*

Carmichael, A., (1900) *Carmina Gadelica*, Volume 1

Carmody, I., (2012) Names of the Dagda https://storyarchaeology. com/names-of-the-dagda/

Cathasaigh, T., (2014) *Coire Sois: The Cauldron of Knowledge a companion to early Irish saga*

Clark, R., (1991) *The Great Queens: Irish Goddesses from the Morrigan to Cathleen ní Houlihan*

Corrigan, I., (2017) Dagda, retrieved from https://www.adf.org/ articles/gods-and-spirits/celtic/dagda.html

Cross and Slover, (1936) *Ancient Irish Tales*

Daimler, M., (2015) *The Treasure of the Tuatha De Danann: A dual language collection of Irish myth*

Danaher, K., (1972) *The Year in Ireland*

Dúil Dromma Cetta (n.d.) retrieved from http://www.asnc.cam. ac.uk/irishglossaries/

eDIL (n.d.) Electronic Dictionary of the Irish Language

Ellis, P., (1994) *Dictionary of Celtic Mythology*

Ellis, P., (1999) *Celtic Myths and Legends*

Estyn Evans, E., (1957) *Irish Folk Ways*

Fraser, J., (1916) *The First Battle of Moytura*

Gray, E., (1983) *Cath Maige Tuired*

Green, M., (1992) *Dictionary of Celtic Myth and Legend*

Guyonvarc'h, C., (1999) *The Making of a Druid: Hidden Teachings from the Colloquy of Two Sages*

Gwynn, E., (1924) *Metrical Dindshenchas*, Volume IV

Keating, G., (1634) *Foras Feasa ar Erinn*

Kelly, F., (1988) *A Guide to Early Irish Law*

Koch, J., and Carey, J., (2003) *The Celtic Heroic Age*

Kondratiev, A., (1997) Basic Celtic Deity Types, retrieved from http://www.imbas.org/articles/basic_celtic_deity_types.html

Leahy, A., (1906) *Heroic Romances of Ireland*

Lehmann, R., and Lehmann, W., (1975) *An Introduction to Old Irish*

MacAlister, R., (1941) *Lebor Gabála Érenn*, Part IV

MacDevitt, W., (2009) *The Gallic Wars*

Martin, S., (2008) *The Names of the Dagda*

MacNeill, M., (1962) *The Festival of Lughnasa*

McNeill, F., (1956) *The Silver Bough*, Volume 1

McCone, K., (2000) *Pagan Past and Christian Present in Early Irish Literature*

Meyer, K., (1906) *Triads of Ireland*

O Cathasaigh, T., (2014) *Coire Sois*

O hOgáin, D., (2006) *The Lore of Ireland*

Puhvel, J., (1987) *Comparative Mythology*

Quin, E., (1983) *Dictionary of the Irish Language Based Mainly on Old and Middle Irish Materials*

Ross, A., (1967) *Pagan Celtic Britain*

Ross, A., (1970) *Pagan Celts*

Sanas Cormaic (n.d.) Retrieved from http://www.asnc.cam.ac.uk/irishglossaries/

Sayers, William (1988) 'Cerrce, an Archaic Epithet of the Dagda, Cernnunos, and Conall Cernach', *The Journal of Indo-European Studies*

Schot, R., Newman, C., and Bhreathnach, E., (2011) *Landscapes of Cult and Kingship*

Sjoestedt, M., (2000) *Celtic Gods and Heroes*

Smyth, D., (1988) *A Guide to Irish Mythology*

Stokes, W., and Windisch, E., (1897) *Irische Texte*

Stokes, W., (1891) *The Second Battle of Moytura*

Waddell, J., (2015) *Archaeology and Celtic Myth*

Williams, M., (2016) *Ireland's Immortals: A History of the Gods of Irish Myth*

We think you will also enjoy…

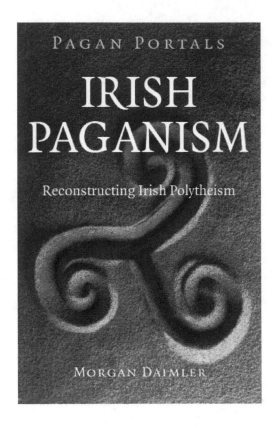

Irish Paganism, Morgan Daimler
Reconstructing Irish Polytheism

...an essential reference for anyone interested in reconstructing the poly-
theist practices of ancient Ireland, and of other Celtic cultures.
Erynn Rowan Laurie

978-1-78535-145-7 (Paperback)
978-1-78535-146-4 (e-book)

Best Selling Pagan Portals & Shaman Pathways

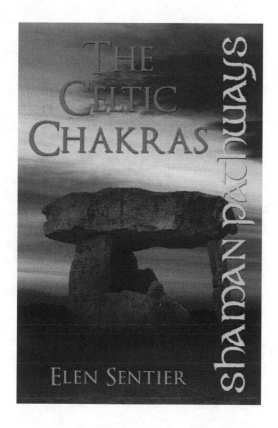

Celtic Chakras, Elen Sentier
Tread the British native shaman's path, explore the Goddess
hidden in the ancient stories; walk the Celtic chakra spiral
labyrinth.

*Rich with personal vision, the book is an interesting exploration of
wholeness*
Emma Restall Orr

978-1-78099-506-9 (paperback)
978-1-78099-507-6 (e-book)

Best Selling Pagan Portals & Shaman Pathways

Druid Shaman, Danu Forest

A practical guide to Celtic shamanism with exercises and techniques as well as traditional lore for exploring the Celtic Otherworld

A sound, practical introduction to a complex and wide-ranging subject
Philip Shallcrass

978-1-78099-615-8 (paperback)
978-1-78099-616-5 (e-book)

Best Selling Pagan Portals & Shaman Pathways

Kitchen Witchcraft, Rachel Patterson
Take a glimpse at the workings of a Kitchen Witch and share in
the crafts

A wonderful little book which will get anyone started on Kitchen
Witchery. Informative, and easy to follow
Janet Farrar & Gavin Bone

978-1-78099-843-5 (paperback)
978-1-78099-842-8 (e-book)

Best Selling Pagan Portals & Shaman Pathways

Moon Magic, Rachel Patterson
An introduction to working with the phases of the Moon

*...a delightful treasury of lore and spiritual musings that should be
essential to any planetary magic-worker's reading list.*
David Salisbury

978-1-78279-281-9 (paperback)
978-1-78279-282-6 (e-book)

Best Selling Pagan Portals & Shaman Pathways

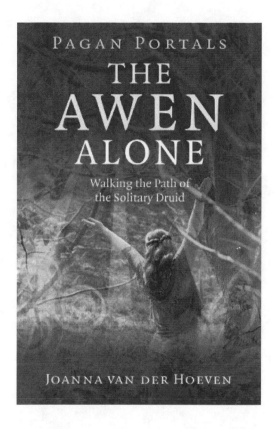

The Awen Alone, Joanna van der Hoeven
An introductory guide for the solitary Druid

Joanna's voice carries the impact and knowledge of the ancestors,
combined with the wisdom of contemporary understanding.
Cat Treadwell

978-1-78279-547-6 (paperback)
978-1-78279-546-9 (e-book)

Best Selling Pagan Portals & Shaman Pathways

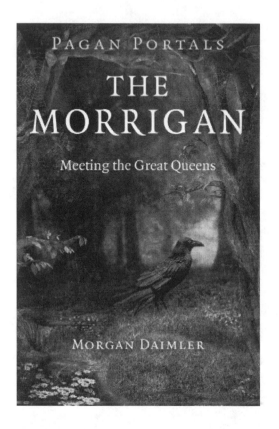

The Morrigan, Morgan Daimler

On shadowed wings and in raven's call, meet the ancient Irish
Goddess of war, battle, prophecy, death, sovereignty, and magic

*...a well-researched and heartfelt guide to the Morrigan from a fellow
devotee and priestess*
Stephanie Woodfield

978-1-78279-833-0 (paperback)
978-1-78279-834-7 (e-book)

PAGANISM & SHAMANISM

What is Paganism? A religion, a spirituality, an alternative belief system, nature worship? You can find support for all these definitions (and many more) in dictionaries, encyclopaedias, and text books of religion, but subscribe to any one and the truth will evade you. Above all Paganism is a creative pursuit, an encounter with reality, an exploration of meaning and an expression of the soul. Druids, Heathens, Wiccans and others, all contribute their insights and literary riches to the Pagan tradition. Moon Books invites you to begin or to deepen your own encounter, right here, right now.

If you have enjoyed this book, why not tell other readers by posting a review on your preferred book site. Recent bestsellers from Moon Books are:

Journey to the Dark Goddess
How to Return to Your Soul
Jane Meredith
Discover the powerful secrets of the Dark Goddess and transform your depression, grief and pain into healing and integration.
Paperback: 978-1-84694-677-6 ebook: 978-1-78099-223-5

Shamanic Reiki
Expanded Ways of Working with Universal Life Force Energy
Llyn Roberts, Robert Levy
Shamanism and Reiki are each powerful ways of healing; together, their power multiplies. *Shamanic Reiki* introduces techniques to help healers and Reiki practitioners tap ancient healing wisdom.
Paperback: 978-1-84694-037-8 ebook: 978-1-84694-650-9

Pagan Portals – The Awen Alone
Walking the Path of the Solitary Druid
Joanna van der Hoeven
An introductory guide for the solitary Druid, *The Awen Alone* will accompany you as you explore, and seek out your own place within the natural world.
Paperback: 978-1-78279-547-6 ebook: 978-1-78279-546-9

A Kitchen Witch's World of Magical Herbs & Plants
Rachel Patterson
A journey into the magical world of herbs and plants, filled with magical uses, folklore, history and practical magic. By popular writer, blogger and kitchen witch, Tansy Firedragon.
Paperback: 978-1-78279-621-3 ebook: 978-1-78279-620-6

Medicine for the Soul
The Complete Book of Shamanic Healing
Ross Heaven
All you will ever need to know about shamanic healing and how to become your own shaman…
Paperback: 978-1-78099-419-2 ebook: 978-1-78099-420-8

Shapeshifting into Higher Consciousness
Heal and Transform Yourself and Our World with Ancient
Shamanic and Modern Methods
Llyn Roberts
Ancient and modern methods that you can use every day to
transform yourself and make a positive difference in the world.
Paperback: 978-1-84694-843-5 ebook: 978-1-84694-844-2

Readers of ebooks can buy or view any of these bestsellers by
clicking on the live link in the title. Most titles are published in
paperback and as an ebook. Paperbacks are available in traditional
bookshops. Both print and ebook formats are available online.

Find more titles and sign up to our readers' newsletter at
http://www.johnhuntpublishing.com/paganism
Follow us on Facebook at https://www.facebook.com/MoonBooks
and Twitter at https://twitter.com/MoonBooksJHP